A TREASURY
OF GREAT PRINTS

A TREASURY OF

GREAT PRINTS

By

IRVIN HAAS

NEW YORK : THOMAS YOSELOFF, INC.

For
IRENE, KARIN, and PETER

FOREWORD

DURING THE FIVE hundred years of print history many of our famous and near-famous artists have found print media particularly suited, in their appeal of immediacy and intimate statement, to their expression. This rich heritage of art should be made accessible to an audience which would be eager to share the esthetic and spiritual experiences inherent in prints if they were aware of this heritage. This book was designed to serve as a visual reminder that such great treasures do exist, and that many of them are within the means of almost everyone to own, contemplate, and enjoy. Unlike paintings in which only a single original exists and consequently becomes a rare and expensive object, prints are a multiple medium of expression. Except for print rarities that have been lost or destroyed by the ravages of time and accident, all prints exist in many proofs of a single subject. Thus, both you and the museum in your city can possess the same print.

In almost a decade of print reviewing, I have seen thousands of etchings, engravings, woodcuts, and lithographs in countless exhibitions and private collections. I have reviewed this vast group in my mind and have judged them by the criteria of creative expression, graphic statement, and technical achievement. The prints I have finally selected for this book are those which have endured in my memory and have given pleasure each time I have returned to them.

I am aware that another critic might make an entirely different selection with equal justification. I make no claim that these are the "best." In a field so rich with treasures it would be patently impossible to select the sixty "best." I have avoided, as much as possible, selecting those perennial favorites that have been reproduced repeatedly. While familiarity does not necessarily need to breed contempt, the unfamiliar is more likely to inspire the exciting and sublime reaction that we should all experience before a work of art.

A great artist creates more than a single masterpiece during a creative lifetime and deserves to be honored for all of them. As time goes on, each work of art becomes part of the life experience of the beholder rather than graphic chapters in the biography of the artist. It is with this goal of personal enrichment in mind that I have selected these prints. They are intended to be seen and enjoyed—not to serve as chronological footnotes for a course in art appreciation.

I want to extend my appreciation to the following who have aided me in this compilation: Dr. Alfred Frankfurter, Editor and Publisher of *Art News;* The Metropolitan Museum of Art; Curt Valentin; Agnes Mongan of The National Gallery; The Wiggin Collection; The Cleveland Museum of Art; The Museum of Modern Art; and George Binet.

IRVIN HAAS

LIST OF PLATES

TECHNIQUE OF THE PRINT

A "PRINT" MUST be distinguished from a piece of reproductive printing because it is the creative result of an artist's own work as opposed to the mechanical result of modern printing. The artist actually makes a design on a metal plate, stone, or block, and frequently prints it as well. The pressman merely prints a plate that has been manufactured by a photographic process. The term "print" covers many techniques, but usually embraces three categories: Relief, Intaglio, and Planographic.

RELIEF PRINTING is done from a surface on which the areas to be printed stand in relief from the block, or, the areas *not* to be printed are cut away, leaving the printed areas *above* the surrounding surface. WOODCUTS fall into this category.

INTAGLIO PRINTING is done from a surface on which the areas to be printed are *not* raised above, but are cut below the surface and the paper is forced into the indentations to print an impression. ETCHINGS and ENGRAVINGS are printed by this method.

PLANOGRAPHIC PRINTING retains the design on the actual printing surface without any difference of level. LITHOGRAPHS fall into this category.

THE RELIEF TECHNIQUES

The WOODCUT is a relief print because the artist, working on a wood block, cuts away the wood on each side of a line in his design, thus leaving the surface of the line raised to receive the ink. The result is a black line on the paper. It is the oldest of all print techniques.

WOOD ENGRAVING is a variation of the relief technique in which the effect is the reverse of the woodcut. The artist cuts lines *into* the wood block so that they will be below the surface of the block. Since the ink is held on the surface and does not penetrate into the incised lines, the lines consequently print as white on a black background.

WOOD BLOCK PRINTING is a color printing process derived from woodcuts. A separate block is cut for each color used. LINOLEUM BLOCK PRINTING is done by exactly the same technique as the woodcut, but the linoleum used is a softer substance than wood, and consequently more pliable and easier to cut.

THE INTAGLIO TECHNIQUES

ETCHING is generally done on a copper plate upon which wax is melted to form a thin coat over the entire surface of the plate. The design is drawn on this thin coat of wax with a sharp-pointed needle. The needle cuts through the wax, exposing the copper plate below. The plate is then placed in a tray containing acid. The wax is impervious to the acid, but the copper is not. Hence, the acid eats into the copper plate wherever it has been exposed by the needle. When the thin wax is removed, what is left is the design *etched* into the copper plate by the action of the acid. Then it is inked and printed.

LINE ENGRAVING is done on a polished metal plate upon which the artist cuts his design directly into the plate with a sharp steel tool called a *burin* or a *graver*. The character of the line is varied by the size of the tool and by the depth of the cut. The plate is then inked and printed. The art of engraving dates from the fifteenth century.

THE PLANOGRAPHIC TECHNIQUE

The LITHOGRAPH is a planographic print because its lines are neither raised in relief nor incised. They are placed directly on the surface. The artist uses a special limestone (zinc and glass have also been used) upon which he draws his design with a greasy crayon. The greasy substance in the crayon adheres to the stone wherever the surface is touched by the crayon. When the drawing or design is finished, the surface of the stone is treated with acid to insure that the greasy substance is permanently fixed. The stone is then sponged with water and rolled with printer's ink. The ink adheres to the greasy substance, but not to the damp stone. A sheet of paper is laid on the dampened and inked stone, and the whole thing is run through the press to produce the lithograph.

There are variations of the above techniques. In some cases artists have mixed various techniques for a single print to produce some special effect. The prints reproduced in this book are examples of all the techniques described.

A TREASURY
OF GREAT PRINTS

MARTIN SCHONGAUER

Angel of the Annunciation

THE ENGRAVING ART is centuries old. It was first used to inscribe ornamentation on metals by goldsmiths and metal-chasers. It was not until the fifteenth century that engraving became a technique employed for the purpose of taking impressions on paper. The early engravers never signed their works, and consequently personal identification of the artist is a matter of speculation. The first known artist to break through this mist of anonymity was Martin Schongauer, the leading German painter-engraver of his time. His distinctive initials, and even more distinctive style, clearly identify the one hundred and fifteen separate plates that comprise his complete known work.

Biographical details on Schongauer are rather sketchy. He was born in Germany in 1430. His father, Casper Schongauer, was a goldsmith who moved with his family to Colmar about 1440. Martin worked in his father's shop as an apprentice and learned the intricacies of his craft there and perhaps in other shops. Like many goldsmiths of the time, he turned to engraving.

Schongauer probably turned to painting early in his career. We know that the work of the Flemish painter Roger van der Weyden was a potent influence, and that only about a half dozen paintings can definitely be attributed to Schongauer although contemporary documents show that he was very active and must have made many more. In his day, the painter was a subordinate artisan who supplied only wings to the great altarpieces which were a prominent feature in the Gothic churches of fifteenth-century Germany. Schongauer achieved recognition beyond these narrow limits assigned to his contemporaries. His painting also had a profound influence on the engravers of his day. Dürer was so impressed with Schongauer's work that he wanted to become his pupil. Schongauer, the last of the medievalists in art, represents the transition between the mannerisms of Late Gothic and the romantic idealism of the German Renaissance which is exemplified by the earthy accents of Dürer.

The engraving *Angel of the Annunciation* is the culmination of Schongauer's art and belongs to his most mature period. It demonstrates his superb rise above the limitations of Gothic achieved by his softening of tortuous contours and his simplification of Gothic conception. This print is a model of simplification because everything not necessary for a clear presentation has been eliminated. The slight shadow upon the ground gives solidity to the figure. The whirling movement of the drapery wrapping the half-kneeling figure in a spiral, and this same movement repeated in the scroll, gives dynamic action to the otherwise immobile figure. There has been much academic argument about the engravings of Schongauer, but all critics agree that this splendid print, probably made shortly before his death in 1491, is his supreme triumph, the engraving that best represents his art.

16

ALBRECHT DÜRER

Saint Eustace

ALBRECHT DÜRER IS a fascinating enigma, and art historians have made many attempts to probe the mind and motives of this most Germanic of German artists. Dürer is uniquely a symbol of his time and place: Germany at the end of the fifteenth and the beginning of the sixteenth century. He matured at a time when two worlds were at war with each other: the pedantic Gothic medievalism that served the Northern countries for decades and the opposing and inexorable sweep from the south of the "New Learning," the Italian Renaissance that heralded the advent of a new humanism. The tremendous inner tensions generated by these powerful and conflicting forces blended in the ideas and the art of Dürer and acted as a catalyst that resulted in great art, profound religiosity, intensive researches, and titanic activity in all branches of the humanities.

Nuremberg, the city of Dürer's birth in 1471, was one of the leading art centers in Germany and housed many of its important art schools. It was a fine atmosphere for maturing a brilliant and inquiring mind.

Like all young artists, Dürer served an apprenticeship and his was spent in the workshop of the well-known artist Wolgemut, where he worked on altarpieces and other art commissions. When he completed his training in 1490, he went on to the publishing centers of Basle and Strassburg, centers of the intellectual and artistic life of the time. A trip to Venice in 1495 brought him in close contact with the ideals of the Renaissance and widened his esthetic horizon. After a second journey to Venice in 1506, he devoted most of his time to engraving and to his scientific and theoretical writings. It was during this period that he created his many print masterpieces. A trip to the Netherlands in 1520 stimulated his interest in portraiture and he drew the leading men of his day, including Erasmus. In the last years of his life his main concern was the publication of his theoretical works which he wished to leave as his intellectual heritage to the world of letters. He died in 1528, leaving a large body of art works of which about one thousand pieces are known to be extant.

Dürer was always inspired by visions of the past ages of Christianity. In the magnificent engraving *Saint Eustace,* he chose his subject from the oft-told tale of the Charitable Eustace, or Placidus, as he was known before his miraculous conversion while hunting. The scene is the psychological moment in the legend when the stag is finally brought to bay. The engraving is filled with pictorial richness—lean, brittle, expressive forms and restless lines. The background landscape reflects Dürer's minute and expert observation of nature: the common native herbs, the plants, flowers, trees, and animals. His engraving technique shows that he had overcome successfully all technical difficulties and was an absolute master of the medium.

HANS BALDUNG GRIEN

Adam and Eve

HANS BALDUNG, CALLED Grien, was one of the most distinctive and vigorous artists of the first half of the sixteenth century. He lived, worked, and strove for recognition in a period that was dominated by two great masters of Germanic art, Albrecht Dürer and Matthias Grünewald. His style and philosophy were rooted in both these giants— in Dürer's great static nature and restless intellectual curiosity, and in the emotional and dynamic spirit of Grünewald, a mystic and an expressionist.

Baldung was born in the small town of Weyersheim near Strassburg about 1480 to 1484. He was born to a learned family, and while still a young man migrated to Nuremberg where he was apprenticed to Dürer, probably for two years beginning in 1507. Later he moved to Freiburg in Breisgau, where he painted an altarpiece for the cathedral. His remaining years were spent in Strassburg, where he died in 1545. Although he worked with and enjoyed a close personal association with Dürer, he is only slightly indebted to him for the formation of his style. It is Grünewald's pictorial and rhapsodic touch that is responsible for the worldly and almost pagan flavor of Baldung's art, a flavor evident in all of his hundreds of drawings, woodcuts, stained glass, paintings, and book illustrations. However, no matter how close he was to Grünewald in temperament, he departed from the mystic's seriousness by touches of superficial elegance and decorative beauty.

It was said that for Baldung the woodcut was the natural language. It exhibits, for one thing, how the professional woodcutters of the period carried over to the block, without much loss of expression, the precise quality of the drawn line. The range of his themes was fascinating. He was capable of portraying deeply religious subjects, and also delighted in presenting erotic witches and lovely female nudes. *Adam and Eve* is a superb combination of both the spiritual and erotic qualities of the artist. It is a sympathetic interpretation of the biblical story of the fall of man, but, at the same time, the sensuousness of the female figure, in spite of the coy fig leaf, is apparent. Eve's expression is as tempting as any of history's most bewitching sirens. The intense psychological expressionism of Baldung is directly reflected in the German Expressionists of the twentieth century.

20

LAPSVS HVMA:
VÎ GENERIS ⁛

NATIONAL GALLERY OF ART

·ER·ROT·

TERMINVS

Corporis effigiem si quis non uidit Erasmi,
Hanc scite ad uiuum picta tabella dabit.

HANS HOLBEIN the Younger

Desiderius Erasmus of Rotterdam

THIS CLASSICAL PORTRAIT of the scholar Erasmus by Holbein the Younger has a two-fold significance: it is a perceptive example of the superb analytical portrait art of one of the three great German artists of the High Renaissance, and it is symbolic of the closing days of a great man's life and the end of his epoch of culture—one of the greatest in European history. The richness of the cultural picture offered by sixteenth-century Northern Europe was the result of religious revolution and reform which affected artistic and intellectual life intensely and led to an artistic renaissance and the movement of Humanism. The chief tenet of Humanism was a new human ideal based on intellectual culture, spiritual freedom, and authority of the personality. Erasmus was one of its greatest exponents and, at the time, the most widely known scholar in the civilized world. He was also the friend and patron of Holbein.

Holbein the Younger was born in Augsburg in 1497, the son of an outstanding painter, Hans Holbein the Elder. The stupendous portrait art of the son had its roots in the wise instruction of the father. At seventeen, Holbein moved to Basle, the cultural center of Europe and the Humanist movement. It was there that he met Erasmus who admired his work and commissioned him to make designs for several of his publications. Holbein quickly became famous for his portraits, altarpieces, frescoes, and designs for stained glass and coats of arms. He also started a series of portraits of Erasmus that continued for the duration of their friendship.

In 1526, Holbein left Basle for England with a letter of introduction from Erasmus to the English philosopher Thomas More who, as his new patron, secured commissions for him. He returned to Basle in 1528, but found it a cultural desert. The movement against Humanism, known as the Reformation, had won its battle and had broken the backbone of German art. Holbein returned to London to stay. He was appointed court painter to Henry VIII and his portraits of the king, his wives and entourage, and the leading English personalities of the day afford ample proof that he was one of the master portrait painters of the sixteenth century. He is the only artist of his period who ranks with Dürer. Holbein died in 1543.

Holbein's last portrait of Erasmus is the woodcut reproduced on the facing page. It is a touching epitaph for the great Humanist. Erasmus stands in the doorway of a rounded Renaissance arch, leaning on his symbol, the herma of Jupiter Terminus. A friend of Erasmus once presented to him a ring with an ancient gem depicting Terminus. Hence, Erasmus chose the Terminus for his emblem and used the stone as a seal. He connected the Terminus with the idea of the limit of all things. Thus Terminus reminded him of the end of life.

PIETER BRUEGEL the Elder

The Journey to Emmaus

FEW WORKS OF art are less in need of commentary than Bruegel's. They are among those rare masterpieces which have had immediate appeal and a widespread acceptance by the people of the artist's own times and through the centuries down to our own. Bruegel's work was mainly concerned with three themes: thinly disguised condemnations of the Inquisition which at the time was crucifying Flanders, robust portrayals of the life of the common folk, and, finally, important innovations in the art of landscape which made him the greatest master of landscape since Bellini.

Bruegel was born in Brabant, Holland, in 1525. At the age of twenty, he went to Antwerp and apprenticed himself to the artist Pieter Coeck. After some years of study he was received into the Painter's Guild of Antwerp in 1551, and then set out upon his *wanderjahre* and gravitated to Italy, where he stayed for two years. He brought back a feeling for Italian style and a knowledge of the fundamentals of Italian art, particularly of their Mannerist style of landscape painting. He went to work for the print publishing establishment of Hieronymous Cock, an astute business man and art critic who had gathered the best artists of the day around him. They and Bruegel supplied him with views, portraits, and moral subjects which were in great demand. Bruegel contributed a considerable number of drawings which were, in turn, copied and etched by anonymous craftsmen and scattered in countless impressions throughout the country. He worked for Cock from 1553 until a few years before his death in 1569.

Bruegel's most popular works are his pictorial records of the daily life of his people. He drew children at play, peasants dancing, farmers at work, weddings, and drinking bouts. These subjects earned him the title of "Droll Peter." He was continuously excited by what he saw, and possessed such prodigious powers of observation and memory that his pictures are the most truthful works of fact in Flemish art. It was in the art of landscape that he produced his most significant expression. He used landscape as a background for all his figures, filling it with a rich accumulation of incidents and a pictorial narration that was in essence a pattern of man's life activity. His engraving *The Journey to Emmaus* is one subject from a series of ten known as the *Grands Paysages*. The series was conceived on his journey to Rome and is typical of the Italian Mannerist style. *The Journey to Emmaus* is a panoramic print in which the essential ingredients of style were borrowed from the Italian originators. They are a high view point, a range of scraggy mountains, and a distant prospect. Bruegel synthesized these elements and added the drama of human life. It is the anecdotal element that inspires our response. In this splendid print the anecdotal element focuses on the back of the Mysterious Pilgrim flanked by two disciples. It is a poetic and profound conception.

EVNTES IN EMAVS

HENDRIK GOLTZIUS

Mars and Venus

THE SECOND HALF of the sixteenth century was a time of intellectual ferment. Scholars and artists traveled freely in Europe absorbing and exchanging ideas and techniques. Culture was international—the same styles that prevailed in Venice were seen in Rome. The dominant style in all countries was Mannerism, a complex style refined to the utmost subtlety. Holland was one of the great art centers of the period with the greatest concentration of artists in Haarlem. Her artists were more outstanding as engravers than painters, and of these the greatest master was Hendrik Goltzius.

Goltzius was born in Muhlbrecht in 1558 and began his career as a painter of small portraits. He became leader of the Mannerist group of artists in Holland, after a short conversion to Classicism, acquired by studying Antique art in Rome in 1590. The flamboyant and elongated forms of Mannerism were particularly suited to the engraving technique and Goltzius underwent an intensive training in the art, emulating the great engravers of the past, Dürer and Lucas van Leyden. He became the greatest engraver of his time. It was a good time for the art and there was great demand for engravings. Dutch and Flemish dealers extended their activities to all of Europe. All the professions had need of prints, and the Church recognized the value of engravings as a subsidiary to secular propaganda. In this fertile atmosphere Goltzius developed his art to its highest pitch and soon had complete command of the entire gamut of technical expression.

He proved his great mastery in the most dazzling display of his competence, *The Masterpieces of Goltzius,* six large plates which duplicated the styles of Raphael, Bassano, Parmigianino, Dürer, and van Leyden. On an equal plane, but in a style entirely his own, is the engraving *Mars and Venus,* typical of the massive figure compositions in which the Mannerists excelled. His dexterity is manifest in every part of the plate. Heavy bulging clouds and a fleecy couch support numerous nudes who elegantly twist and balance, creating a stirring dramatic impact. His forms are vital, alive with many curves that dominate the composition, and are bombastic in effect. There is a great breadth of line work—swelling and diminishing, creating exciting rhythms and expressing tone and surface qualities. The virtuosity displayed in this print has seldom been equaled in the medium at any time.

Goltzius died in Haarlem in 1617, and even at his death the beginning of the end of Mannerism was presaged by the powerful realism of Caravaggio.

JACQUES CALLOT

Jousts of Florence

IT WAS A swaggering cloak-and-dagger France into which Jacques Callot was born in 1592. It was the licentious period immortalized by Dumas *père* in the derring-do of his swaggering Musketeers. It was a cynical, dissolute, and war-torn age that was characterized by Voltaire as "a silken robe smeared with blood."

Callot's own life reads like a story-book version of his times. He was born in Nancy into a family of minor officials at the Court of Duke Henry III of Lorraine. He was intended for the Church but spent his early years in the workshops of artists and craftsmen. Learning about the cultural wonders of Rome, the twelve-year-old Callot ran away from home and headed for Italy. He joined a band of gypsies, left them at Florence, and went on to the Eternal City. Here family friends found him and shipped him back home. His second truancy was less successful; his brother overtook him at the Italian border. His persistence soon forced his parents to consent to his going to Rome to study art. In the years he studied and worked there, he became a master printmaker and won recognition and support from royalty and art patrons.

Callot explored every facet of his society. Each was studied and portrayed by his discerning graver. A complete cross-section of his world can be found in his prints which include as subjects peasants, soldiers, nobles, gypsies, beggars, courtesans, cavaliers, actors, acrobats, street-scenes, battles, the theater and the gaming houses. It is the first graphic portrayal of Western European society at the very birth of modern times.

Callot's graphic conception was always panoramic. He created large and inclusive scenes peopled by hundreds and even thousands of subjects. Each print is crowded with tiny figures in spirited action. He used an aerial view so that the spectator looked down at the scene for a rapid visual summation. The etching *Jousts of Florence* is a splendid example of his dramatic expression. There are hundreds of figures in and around the jousting ring, yet each is modeled with marvelous detail. The composition is so skillful that in no section of the scene is there a feeling of meaningless chaos. Each part of the print is perfectly organized. His aerial perspective weaves distance and atmosphere into a forceful unified composition.

Callot's new and revolutionary visual approach to composition and expression was a precursor of the school of the modern grotesque that influenced such diverse figures as Poe, Kafka, Dali, and de Chirico. Callot lived only forty-two years, but in this short span he immortalized an age and an approach to art, and created a glorious chapter of graphic history.

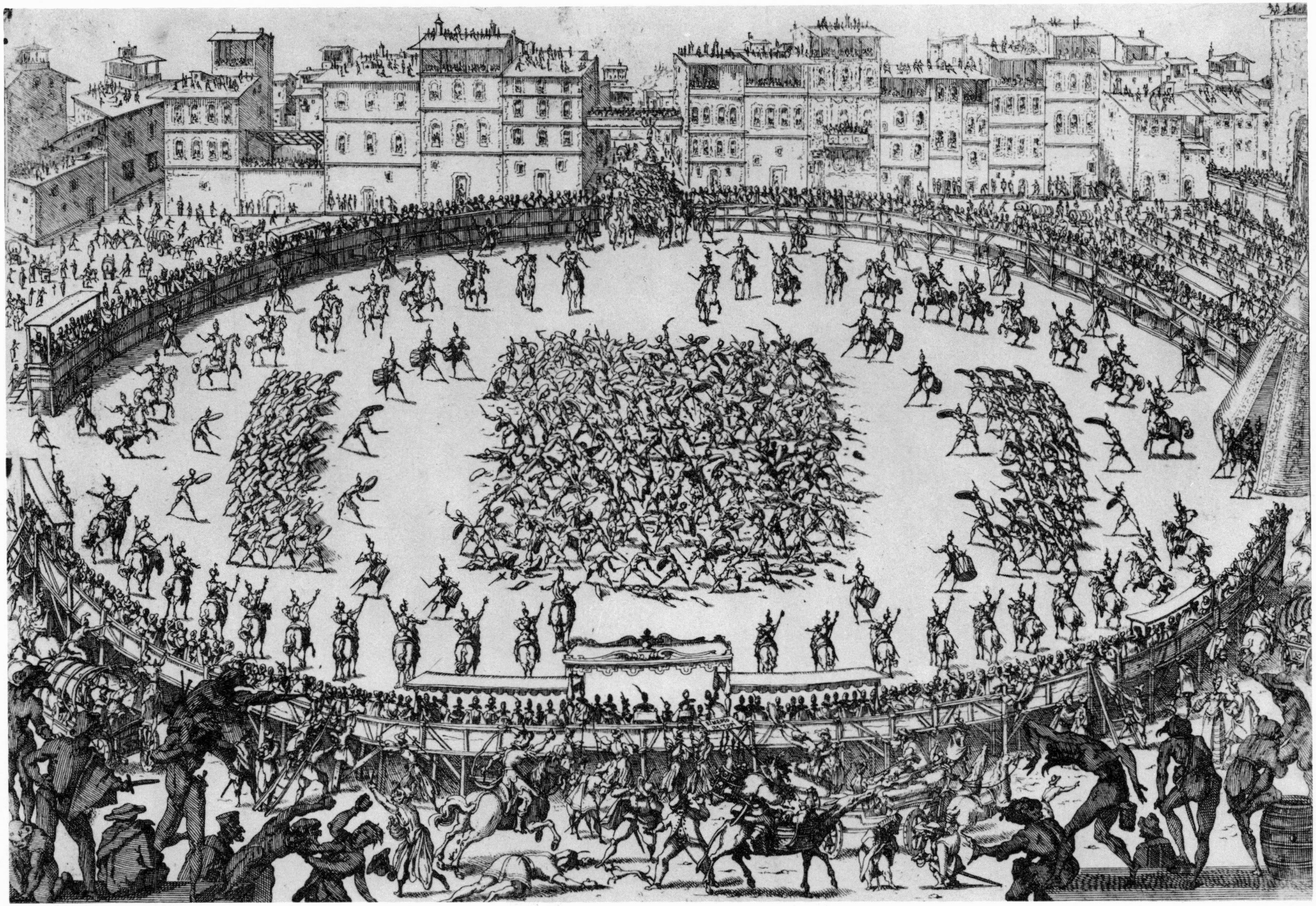

NATIONAL GALLERY OF ART

Philipe Le Roy.

ANTON VAN DYCK

Philipe le Roy

IT IS DOUBTFUL whether any artist other than Van Dyck has ever made such an illustrious reputation with so small a number of prints. Only eighteen plates are attributed to him, but each is among the most beautiful and accomplished portraits ever made in etching. They are as elegant as their creator, who was the darling of royal society and could have sat for one of his own sparkling portraits to be entitled "The Fashionable Portrait Painter." He was as cavalier as his patrons. His studio was magnificent, hung with Old Masters and serviced by numerous pupils and assistants. He entertained sumptuously and was as much at home in the glittering court of his patron Charles I as he was at his own easel.

Van Dyck is listed as a Flemish painter only because of origin. His best work was done in Italy and England. Born in 1599, he was admitted to the Antwerp Guild of Painters in 1618, and a year later entered the studio of Rubens. He soon became the most talented pupil in that vast art factory and absorbed much of his master's style and technique. He was invited to England by James I, where he painted portraits for three months and then went on to Italy. He remained in Italy for several years absorbing the work of the Venetian masters, particularly Titian, and painting portraits of the Genoese nobility. When he returned to England in 1632, he was at the height of his powers and he accepted the title of Court Painter to Charles I. The pomp and glitter of that art-loving monarch's Court was the perfect surrounding for Van Dyck. Art and a penchant for opulent decorative effects in décor and costume were very popular, and Van Dyck was ideally suited to exploit this material. He was still exploiting it superbly when he died nine years later.

Van Dyck takes full rank with the great masters of portrait art. He gave the world of fashion that posed for him an elegance, beauty, and distinction which no other period can equal. He brought to perfection the type of portrait that came into demand in English society in the seventeenth century and remained popular to the time of Sargent. His influence was not only strong in England, but on the continent as well. Nor was it restricted to his own time, for it inspired the eighteenth-century painters.

The etched portrait *Philipe le Roy* is one of the brilliant analytical delineations typical of Van Dyck's courtly conceptions. It is a problem in dramatic personification and the sitter served him as a peculiarly well-organized manikin to be forced into the shape and form of a distinguished predilection. Within its limitations of form and intention it is perfect. His etching technique is economical and done with great felicity of line. It has that same cool silvery quality, that languid ease of execution, that made all of Van Dyck's etchings the much sought-after treasures of the print-maker's art.

REMBRANDT VAN RIJN

The Woman with the Arrow

THE SEVENTEENTH CENTURY in Dutch history was crowded with many great and near-great artists. The times were prosperous and propitious for patronage. The young Dutch nation had just ended its struggle for independence, and a successful peace brought confidence and rapid growth in the land. It was a time of rich living and lush social intercourse; it was the Holland reflected in the paintings of Frans Hals, materialistic and Philistine, with little concern for the spiritual aspects of life. Rembrandt towered above the contemporary art of commonplace anecdotes and trivial realism with his magnificent paintings and prints. His was an art of deeply poetic imagination and great spiritual significance.

Rembrandt was born in Leyden in 1606, the son of a miller and a baker's daughter. He was destined for a scholar's career but decided instead to study art. His genius was soon recognized in Leyden and he went on to the wealthy Dutch capital of Amsterdam where fortune favored him again with rich portrait commissions, a large house filled with pupils, and a new bride, Saskia van Uylenburgh, daughter of a patrician family.

Perhaps his youthful successes were too rapid and too heady. The frenzied mercantile atmosphere of Amsterdam did not make for stability and he soon overextended himself financially. Then, too, the more elegant portrait style of Van Dyck was coming into fashion, and the popularity of Rembrandt's more dramatic Baroque style suffered and he lost his commissions. As a final stroke, his adored wife, Saskia, whom he immortalized in hundreds of prints, paintings and drawings died, and he suffered complete collapse.

This piling up of misfortunes seemed after a time to have a purifying effect. He turned to etching as a more intimate medium for his expression. The editions he printed also allowed him a livelihood because they were bought not only in the Netherlands but all over Europe and soon became sought after by artists and collectors. His portraits, biblical subjects, and landscapes exhibited an emotional expressiveness, a dramatic mastery, and a technical skill that still stands out pre-eminently among all artistic skills developed since his death.

The *Woman with the Arrow* was the last of Rembrandt's dated etchings, and one of the rarest and most graceful of all his nude studies. The masterful play of light over the body and the couch, highlighting dramatic areas with astute pictorial staging, show Rembrandt to be one of the greatest masters of chiaroscuro in the history of printmaking. We do not know the symbolic significance of the arrow the woman is holding aloft. It may be there for narrative effect, for Rembrandt was the finest story-teller who has yet worked in black-and-white, and this wonderful print is a combination of all the many facets of his great talents.

NATIONAL GALLERY OF ART

WILLIAM HOGARTH

The Laughing Audience

ENGLAND IN HOGARTH'S day was a frenzied stage of glaring contrasts. Its middle class—industrious, aspiring, and conservative—was about to launch the great agrarian and technical revolution that would make Britain the most prosperous country in Europe. But of its seven million population, one million lived jammed in the twelve-mile area of Greater London—a shameful cesspool of sin, corruption, and squalor. There was much idleness, disease, and crime; much drinking, dueling, gambling, wenching, and murders. It was this robust kaleidoscope of social and economic ferment that Hogarth recorded and interpreted with humor, irony, and passion.

William Hogarth, the son of a schoolmaster, was born in London in 1697. His childhood can best be described in his own words: "As I had naturally a good eye and a fondness for drawing, *shows* of all sorts gave me uncommon pleasure. An early access to a neighboring painter drew my attention from play; and I was, at every possible opportunity, employed in making drawings." At the age of fifteen, he was apprenticed to a silverplate engraver and learned to engrave on copper. At the age of twenty-three he set himself up as an independent engraver and his career started. From the first he had an all-absorbing interest in contemporary life and found the popular manner of realistic story-telling the most appropriate form for his art. His interests were all-embracing—life at the Court, in the great houses and the garrets, in park and slum. There were few aspects of English life that his questing pencil did not record. His sense of satire was unerring, always edged by an energetic cockney humor that earned him early popularity. His monumental series of engravings, *The Harlot's Progress, The Rake's Progress,* and *Marriage à la Mode,* attracted a wide and eager audience. His morality was simple: men seek in vain to live in luxury without work, idleness leads to disaster, industry is rewarded. These were the values of the middle class and Hogarth was their graphic spokesman. He died in 1764, honored as one of the great masters of English art.

The Laughing Audience is an ingratiating etching that epitomizes the informal comic streak in his work. It also reflects the very apt title his contemporaries bestowed upon Hogarth, "The Cockney's Mirror," for certainly this very busy scene mirrors an amazing range of facial expressions from convulsed laughter to bored indifference. The background couples, oblivious to the stage, are absorbed in lusty love-play. One can almost hear the program vendor hawking her wares to the inattentive lovers. The technique and expression are typical of Hogarth's methods. He used the scenic artist's device for articulating and emphasizing the dramatic action of his figures. His set is solid, clearly bounded and outlined, and of a box-like compactness. His highlights are dispersed over the entire composition to pick out its sub-plots. It is one of the most entertaining and perceptive prints in Hogarth's great body of graphic art.

35

GIOVANNI BATTISTA PIRANESI

Carceri—Plate XIII

PIRANESI WAS THE self-appointed pictorial historian of the antiquities of ancient Rome. He was an irascible and unpredictable genius whose overwhelming output of enormous plates was as remarkable for sheer number as for quality. His contemporaries begrudgingly referred to him as the "Rembrandt of the Ruins" and the "prodigious Piranesi." He dedicated his entire life and extraordinary talents to recording the moldering records of past Roman glories, combining great art and archeological scholarship in his creations.

Piranesi's single-minded purpose was all the more amazing when viewed in the light of his times. It was an age of frivolities. The upper class Italian of that day was forced to limit himself to an idle, purposeless existence, concerned only with petty issues and problems. In this listless world, the genius of Piranesi towered above his contemporaries.

Piranesi was born in Venice in 1720, the son of a mason. His maternal uncle was an architect and engineer, and was responsible for shaping his nephew's mind and his veneration for architecture. Piranesi's region produced almost all of the great Italian architects since Michelangelo, and young Giovanni followed tradition in studying architecture with various masters. His violent temper finally alienated all his teachers and his uncle, and self-study became his sole training. His readings from ancient history fired him with an ambition to go to Rome, and he finally got his chance by being taken as a draughtsman on the staff of the new Venetian ambassador to the Vatican. The Eternal City opened a new world to him which centered in the imperial ruins. He knew at once that this was henceforth to become his only world. He learned the art of etching as the most personal and immediate medium to pictorialize the many crumbling ruins that literally littered Rome. His poverty was great, but his unswerving purpose and labors were unceasing and tireless. He produced a new plate about every two weeks and a monumental book of plates every two years. Though his reputation grew as an artist, he remained a poor man all of his life. The tremendous cost of producing so many plates was never balanced by the sales. When he died in Rome in 1778, he left his family little but great stacks of plates.

The *Carceri* is his finest series, and, peculiarly enough, solely the product of his intense imagination. These sixteen fantasies were done at the age of twenty-two and published when he was thirty. They represent interiors of vast and fantastic architecture, filled with a complexity of vaulting arches, grim engines of torture, and massive piers. Little bodies of humans in chains are dwarfed in dark and dramatic immensities of space. Slim ladders, scaffoldings, and bridges traverse the delirium of arches and foundations, bathed in eerie half-lights. The *Carceri* are perhaps the first approaches to abstract art emanating from the eighteenth century.

FRANCISCO JOSÉ DE GOYA Y LUCIENTES

Divided Bull Ring

No OTHER ARTIST in black-and-white has ever exhibited the tremendous vitality, the seething indignation, and the wealth of symbolism of Francisco José de Goya y Lucientes. In all of his work there is an exuberant, full-bodied delight in life, a fierce hatred for sham and injustice, and an overflow of sheer animal spirits tempered by the wit and wisdom of a great creativity.

Goya lived, as we do, in the confusion and tumult of a prewar, war, and postwar time. The tensions and insecurity of his time weighed upon him and his contemporaries. His was a world strewn with disasters, treasons, and intrigues—a world to which only a satirist could do full justice, and Goya was the greatest graphic satirist of all time.

He was born in the region of Aragon in Spain in 1746 and died in exile at Bordeaux in 1828. Between these years his life and career swept in a stormy and adventurous current. He was physically powerful enough to survive more than eighty years of an uncommonly strenuous life, sportsman enough to have been an excellent amateur bullfighter and to have crossed the Pyrenees alone on a mule at the age of eighty; he was lusty enough to have had innumerable love affairs and to have sired twenty legitimate children; and he was genius enough to have immortalized his people and his times in the greatest body of art ever produced in Spain.

Goya began his career as a portraitist, but soon became the painter of humanity rather than humans. He castigated his world in his bitter series *The Disasters of War* with savage and unforgettable scenes of rapine and slaughter, and in the series *The Proverbs* with its bizarre symbolism and cryptic reference. The conception and technique of these prints have influenced artists from Delacroix and Manet down to our present day. Goya has been called "the first of the great moderns."

Goya returned to his most beloved sport, bullfighting, again and again. He began recording the exploits and personalities of the bull ring in his series of etchings *The Tauromaquia,* and at the very end of his life he completed his graphic record with a set of four lithographs known as the *Bulls of Bordeaux.* Goya discovered the lithographic process late in life and embraced it eagerly. The lithograph *Divided Bull Ring,* one of the Bordeaux series, is accepted as one of the earliest masterpieces of lithography. It was made by Goya in his eightieth year when he was deaf and almost blind. In this print he left the sins and sadness of the world behind him and returned to the joyous vitality and excitement of his first love—the bull ring. It is a sentimental journey of an old and lonely man. He had lived a long and stormy life and had given it a timeless eloquence through his great art.

FRANCISCO JOSÉ DE GOYA Y LUCIENTES

The Giant

IT IS ENTIRELY fitting that a romantic story be attached to a print by so romantic a figure as Goya. *The Giant* was comparatively unknown to the public and even to art authorities until some twenty years ago. At that time, three of the greatest museums in the world had what each thought was the only impression. Then, another print, now in the collection of the Metropolitan Museum of Art, was found in the Thieves Market in Paris. The publicity resulting from this discovery brought the print at last to the public's attention. The years of oblivion and the dramatic reappearance of the fourth copy of this print show that romance is ever possible in the world of art.

This plate, which is believed to have cracked after the fourth finished proof was pulled, is Goya's only experiment in the mezzotint manner. Because he worked on the plate like a painter brushing white over a dark canvas, he was able to give the print a breadth, majesty, and emotional power equaled only in his greatest paintings.

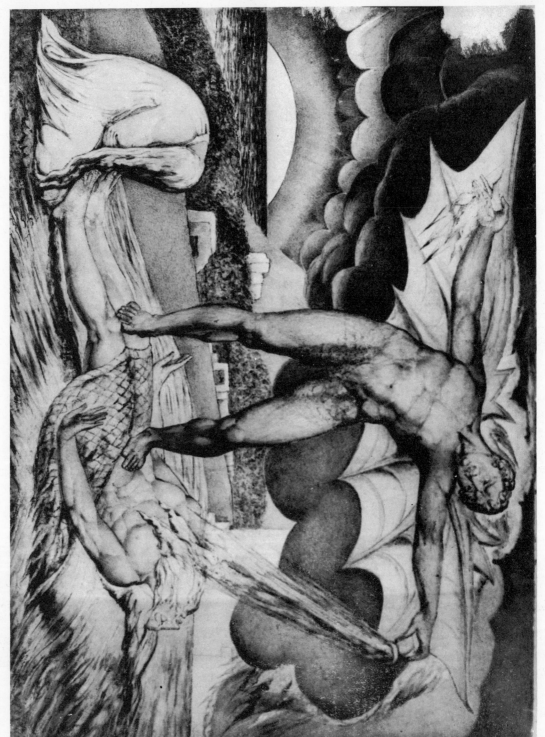

WILLIAM BLAKE

Satan Smiting Job

POET, PHILOSOPHER, PROPHET, and artist, William Blake is one of the most complex and perplexing personalities in the long history of art. Portrayed at various times as an impractical visionary, a madman, a clear-headed thinker, a mystic, and a seer, Blake was probably a bit of all of these. He believed himself to be the chosen instrument to rectify the evils of his society by his art. He lived in troubled times—a period of wars, revolutions, and reactions against revolutions. Like his contemporaries—Shelley, Godwin and Thomson—he believed that only poets and artists were capable of being "the institutors of laws and founders of civil society, and the teachers and inventors of the arts of life." He wrote a magnificent series of *Prophetic Books,* filled with obscure symbolism and allusions, in which he sought to define the systems by which man could create a moral world where the natural creative powers of mankind were in harmony. Blake's art was a graphic extension of his writings, an attempt to combine the greatest intensity of subjective thought and feeling with the greatest clarity of objective representation.

Born in London in 1757, Blake was the son of a dissenter who read Swedenborg and was a hosier by profession. As a child he was nervous and was never sent to school. When he was fourteen he was apprenticed to an engraver, where for the next seven years he learned that craft well enough to support himself for the rest of his life. From that time on until he was thirty, he was a professional engraver, reproducing other artists' work onto metal for book illustration. When he was thirty he devoted himself entirely to creative work. His famous poems, *Songs of Innocence* and *Marriage of Heaven and Hell,* as well as his *Prophetic Books,* are among the many works for which he engraved illustrations. At times, when money was scarce, he again made illustrations for other people's books. When he was more comfortable financially, he developed his system of color printing which he used to print his own writings. In his last years he was surrounded by an appreciative group of young disciples who collected his work and aided him financially—a recognition long due him. Blake died serenely at the age of seventy.

The engraving *Satan Smiting Job* is one of the series Blake engraved for *The Book of Job* in which dramatic line is combined with the most delicate stipple to produce a grandeur of presentation. This scene of Satan smiting Job with sore boils is surprisingly small for so great a theme. In his book Blake gave the engravings added beauty and stature by surrounding each with a decorative border and texts. Although this plate and others in the same series are not exclusively true to his mental vision—as are, for example, his plates for *The Divine Comedy*—they represent a great technical mastery of the burin and a complete domination of his material.

JEAN AUGUSTE DOMINIQUE INGRES

Odalisque

THE CLOSE OF the eighteenth century was one of those well-defined epochs in which the currents of French life influenced and fashioned the currents of her art. The Revolution unleashed emotional forces that swept away the ideals of previous generations. In their place it bred a fierce and almost primitive love for the French people and soil which artists expressed in huge paintings glorifying France's national past.

The men who made the Revolution were educated men steeped in the classics of literature and art. Dissatisfied with their own world, they tried to seize on the ready-made forms of a perfect past which history presented so enticingly. This drive to break away from the present, and to set up in its place a historically accurate reconstruction of some noble past era, was the basis of Classicism. This retreat to the past molded the greatest of the Classic painters, Jacques Louis David. It also helped shape his most famous and talented disciple, Ingres, who represents the beginning of the modern academic tradition and the end of Classicism. An unbroken line leads from him to Degas, Renoir, Lautrec, and Picasso.

Ingres was born at Montauban in 1780. His father was a sculptor and miniature painter who encouraged his son's interest in art. Ingres went to Paris to study with David, and when he was twenty-one, he was awarded the Prix de Rome. He went to Italy and stayed for fourteen years. In the interim the scene in France had changed and artists were clamoring for a new leader to replace David. When Ingres returned he was acclaimed by all and became the leader of the Classical school. He was made a member of the Institute and was awarded the Legion of Honor. He also became the irreconcilable opponent of Delacroix, the founder of the new movement of Romanticism. Ingres was so incensed against the Romanticists' rugged style of painting that he declared all Romantic painters guilty of treason to the state. In 1834 he returned to Italy as Director of the French Academy in Rome. He amassed many more honors, becoming a Senator, a Grand Officer of the Legion of Honor, and France's most celebrated painter of the day. He died in 1867 when he was eighty-seven.

Although Ingres created few prints during his lifetime, printmaking should have been his true métier. Essentially his paintings are faultless drawings, because line rather than color was his major concern. He carried the linear tradition to its highest point of achievement. And printmaking is a linear art. His lithograph *Odalisque*, based on a previous painting, is a miracle of calligraphic expression and plastic contour. The soft, sinuous grace of this Classic nude is saved from the typical convention of the idealized nude by the enchantment of its living line and suave outlines. *Odalisque* proved that the medium of the print was the perfect vehicle for Ingres' expression, for in it he attained a rare perfection.

44

Ingres 1842.   N. plat. de Dupont.

ODALISQUE.

JEAN BAPTISTE CAMILLE COROT

Le Petit Berger

THE ORIGINS OF modern French landscape had their roots in the work of Corot, a dedicated, gentle, and generous man whose entire world was bounded by art and nature. His single-minded faithfulness to these was the key to his success and isolation, and allowed him to be true to himself artistically. Like others of his day he was affected by the thoughts and writings of Rousseau, which stressed man's identification with nature and consequently enriched man's capacity to enjoy the landscape around him. The formal, meticulous scenes of the Classical landscapists were too polished and awesome for personal rapport, and artists like Corot, Diaz, and Daubigny freed themselves from the stereotypes of the Classicists and developed a new Naturalism, an informal, spontaneous, and sketchlike approach to nature that met with instant popular approval and placed landscape in a position of equality with the other genres formerly considered superior.

Corot was born in Paris in 1796, the son of a hairdresser and a milliner. In his youth he worked as a draper and spent all of his spare time painting and drawing. When he was twenty-six, his father settled a small allowance on him and permitted him to devote himself entirely to art. He spent most of his time in the country north of Paris painting landscapes from nature. In 1825 he went to Italy, where he stayed for three years. The landscape sketches he made on this first Italian journey are among his most remarkable. The forms and color of the Italian landscape threw him into a state of passionate receptivity, and this excitement shook him into a freedom of handling that was brilliant. On his return he painted mostly at Fontainebleau. He exhibited regularly at the Salon. In 1838 the Duc d'Orleans bought two of his pictures and from that time on he was recognized, honored, and successful. He became a rich man, but still continued to live simply and quietly, helping many fellow artists who were in need of support. He died in Paris in 1875, mourned by many people for his great art and his greater humanity.

Corot began to etch at the suggestion of some of his friends. His technique was instinctive, and this instinct that served him so well in his painting, served him equally well in etching. His spontaneity resulted in a great decision of stroke and an ability to place the values in their true position. Although most of his etchings were done from memory, their emotional force has not diminished. "In my heart and eyes I preserve a copy of every one of my works," he said. The lovely etching *Le Petit Berger* (The Little Nymph), was probably done from memory or from some sketch for a painting, but no technical difficulty blocked its magnificent rediscovery in his mind. Every stroke has meaning and the restrained scale of values is maintained in the entire plate. The figure is sharply cut and the light filters through the foliage and gives a scintillating play to the print.

47

FERDINAND VICTOR EUGÈNE DELACROIX

La Juive d'Alger

IT WAS SAID that Delacroix had twenty different ways of saying "mon cher monsieur," and each was said to be equally obnoxious to the receiver. He was a reserved and aristocratic man of bewildering complexity. This contradictory man brought a genius and vitality to French art that were of Renaissance proportions and turned the currents of that art from the austere Classicism of David and Ingres to Romanticism, a movement that directed art to personal emotion and the literary subjects of tragic grandeur and death.

His brilliant and unconventional use of light and color and the new techniques he evolved roused the indignation of the Classicists to fever pitch, but inspired the younger generation of artists to emulate his color harmonies and violent compositions. He took his subject matter from romantic poetry and novels, from Shakespeare and the Middle Ages, but principally from the Orient. He was one of the first and greatest Orientalists and introduced the Orient as a popular theme in nineteenth-century French painting. The etching *La Juive d'Alger* is a result of the ideas and impressions he gathered on a trip to Morocco.

Even Delacroix' birth is surrounded in a romantic and mysterious haze. He was born near Paris in 1798. His mother was the daughter of the cabinetmaker to Louis XVI, but there is doubt that his father, Charles Delacroix, was in fact his real father. Rumor gave that honor to the wily politician Talleyrand. He was educated at the Lycée Imperial and joined the studio of Pierre Guerin in 1816. He did not have to wait long for recognition, for his first painting was acquired by the Louvre at the Salon of 1822. He received many commissions and won France's most coveted art honors during his lifetime. He believed that the career of an artist called for isolation and the sacrifice of nearly all the feelings which inspire ordinary men. He never married and had few alliances with women. He continued to paint until his death in Paris in 1863.

The etching *La Juive d'Alger* is more than a memento of his travels. It is a great print in its own right. The details of the composition, the grouping of the figures, the light and shade of foreground and background all show the fruits of his careful study of Goya's powerful style. The voluptuousness and languor of the women that overlays the nervous intensity of their pose creates an air of suspense and the feeling of approaching violence, preceded by just the fleeting moment of contemplative silence. Baudelaire described this elusive quality in Delacroix as "the crater of a volcano, artistically hidden by bouquets of flowers." The vital force of this lithograph, generated by a dramatic chiaroscuro and composition, attests to his well known enthusiasm for printmaking and the great prints he has given us.

48

HONORÉ DAUMIER

Deux Voleurs

THE MODEST AND unassuming Honoré Daumier was an uncomfortable phenomenon to the critics and collectors of his day. They could not categorize him. He would not fit neatly into any of their designated niches. He was a political and social satirist who contributed his picture to the daily comic press. But was this Art? He portrayed and pilloried a society as no artist—with the possible exceptions of Hogarth, Goya, and Rowlandson—had done before. He created more than four thousand lithographs during his more than forty active years. He saw deeply into the mind and spirit of the city-dweller and raised him from the particular to the universal. The critics and collectors admitted that he was the greatest caricaturist of his time. But could such art that was the daily fare of the common man be placed in the sacred Pantheon of Great Artists? Hardly!

Fellow artists and a few friendly critics recognized the fact that Daumier was a superb technician who drew movement and light and masses with consummate skill and graphic power. His line was the most intelligent and forceful of all French art of the period. Such artists as Delacroix, Manet and Degas were influenced by his work and he was praised and honored by Baudelaire, Champfleury and the Goncourts. But collectors could not tolerate an artist who devoted his talents to ridiculing the bourgeoisie. In an age given to loud and vehement pronouncements on art, he set down what he thought in his pictures.

Daumier was born in Marseilles in 1808. His father was a minor poet who depended upon his son's financial support just as soon as he was old enough to go out and work. Honoré worked for a bailiff, a notary and a bookseller, and then turned to his talents for sketching to earn his family a livelihood. He went to work for Charles Philipon, editor and proprietor of *La Caricature* and *Charivari*, who took him on his staff in 1832 and employed him for forty years. During that long time Daumier's graphic satire spanned many regimes—through Empire, Restoration, Chartre, July Monarchy, Republic, Empire, Commune, and into the Third Republic. He was a merciless critic of all. In 1860 his eyesight began to fail and ten years later he became totally blind. He would have died completely destitute if his friend Corot had not helped him and given him a house where he lived until his death in 1879.

In *Deux Voleurs*, or *The Donkey and the Two Thieves*, we witness a highway robbery. Daumier set his struggling antagonists and the fleeing thief on the donkey so expertly in space that the eye travels to all focal points in the succession the artist planned. His use of dramatic line is superb. Notice the expressive curve of the fighter's arms, the ferocity on the half-hidden face, and the stark landscape that acts as a dramatic backdrop. It is a stirring and dynamic composition, a truly great print.

HONORÉ DAUMIER

Rue Transnonain

IN A MOST perceptive essay on Daumier, William M. Ivins, Jr., wrote: "There are two kinds of great artists, those who only produce great works of art and those who profoundly influence the thought and work of their contemporaries and of their successors." There are few artists who have had so great an influence on both their own and succeeding generations as Daumier. The artists of his day grew up with his work constantly before them. Delacroix, Manet, and Degas all knew his work by heart. He not only influenced the art of his day, but the thought as well, for his lithographs appeared in the periodical press two or three times a week for more than forty years. His graphic comments on the day's issues fashioned public opinion. Here was the unique and satisfying spectacle of a great artist whose work reached multitudes frequently enough for them to realize that this day-to-day art was as great and lasting as all the art immured in museums and collections.

The lithograph *Rue Transnonain* was made in 1834, two years after Daumier joined the staff of *Charivari*. During this period a large number of leading Republicans had been imprisoned in connection with the April riots in Paris and Lyon. This horrifying scene of senseless slaughter and fratricide was one of the last scathing indictments that Daumier was able to make for a long time, for that same year the infamous "September Laws" were passed checking all political caricature. The scene shows the dramatic intensity and the amazing control of black-and-white that Daumier possessed.

CHARLES MERYON

La Galerie Notre Dame

THE FALLIBILITY OF public judgment recurs at least once in every generation with devastating results. In the generation of Whistler, Manet, and Bracquemond its pathetic victim was Charles Meryon, a great etcher, a haunted paranoiac, and a poverty-ridden man who would have been glad to sell any of his prints for the price of a meal at any time during his short life. He was not entirely without recognition, for men like Victor Hugo, Baudelaire, and Bracquemond wrote extravagantly of his genius; but collectors and museum committees, unable to recognize some of the finest architectural etching ever done and the most magnificent pictorial record of Old Paris ever presented by a single artist, would not touch his prints.

Meryon was born in Paris in 1821, the illegitimate son of an English doctor and a French ballet dancer. His father neglected him, but his mother watched over his education, and at her death left him twenty thousand francs. He entered the Navy at seventeen, went to sea as a cadet, and became a lieutenant. Ill health forced him to resign his commission in 1846, and he took a studio in Paris, resolved to become a painter. His color-blindness turned his efforts to black-and-white and he studied etching technique with Eugène Blery. But his real master was Reinier Zeeman, a Dutch etcher of the seventeenth century whose views of the Paris of his day inspired Meryon to undertake the great project of his life, the series *Etchings of Paris*. At that time Baron Haussmann was ruthlessly demolishing the picturesque labyrinths of old Paris to replace them with modern streets and boulevards. Meryon was horrified at this destruction and devoted all of his time to recording the ancient buildings and landmarks before they disappeared. His great plates were unsold. The daily lack of food and art materials, sickness and discouragement drove him deeper into mental illness. He wandered the streets of Paris in deep melancholia, feeling a malevolent spirit at large, and buildings and walls ruled over him like flying demons. In a fit of frenzy he destroyed his finest plates, and his behavior became so erratic that he had to be hospitalized in a mental institution from 1858 to 1859. In spite of increasing insanity, his work remained authoritative and unique. His plates showed a great sense of scale, directness of treatment, and brilliant composition. He succeeded in transferring his own intense personality to the very stone walls he etched. Peace only came to the poor and frenzied Meryon when he died in February, 1868.

La Galerie Notre Dame, dated 1853, was made before Meryon's work showed signs of his mental illness. It is a monumental conception of towering verticals in which his directness of treatment is reflected in the precise renditions of texture of old stones. In both these prints the interplay of dark and light instills poetry and intensity in the inanimate objects. In the words of Victor Hugo: "With nothing save shadows and light, it lives, radiates, and thinks. What he does is superb."

CHARLES MERYON

Le Stryge

ONE OF MERYON's most articulate and enthusiastic admirers was the poet Baudelaire who wrote favorably about his work and showed his etchings to influential friends. It was a strange association. The work of both these artists was inspired by a powerful and somber imagination fed by morbid and bizarre fantasy. But in solidity of construction and exquisite technique, their work equals and perhaps excels the work of the best-balanced and sanest of their contemporaries. In summing up Meryon's work, Baudelaire stated: "In the severity, the fineness, and the certainty of his design, Meryon recalls that which was best in the etchers of antiquity."

His etching *Le Stryge,* a study of one of the gargoyles on Notre Dame, illustrates Meryon's minute, punctilious realism which nevertheless retains an eerie, suspenseful quality that combines representation with hallucination. His strong, firm strokes seem to turn the stone to bronze, and his deeply bitten furrows create tonal patterns that keep the immobile sculpture alive and moving.

56

Insatiable vampire, l'eternelle Luxure —
Sur la Grande Cite convoite sa pature.

ÉDOUARD MANET

The Gypsies

THE HISTORY OF French art is particularly rich in daring innovators who diverted standard and accepted streams of art into new and exciting channels. In the early 1860's it was Courbet, a powerful and gifted vulgarian who had revolted against the smooth grace of the Ingres tradition and founded the vital Realist movement. The Realists contended that all fragments of life, no matter how unsavory, were materials for art and that the artist must record them impersonally and scientifically because the recorded fragments were more important than the state of mind or emotional condition of the artist. As Courbet devoted more and more time to politics, his place was taken by Édouard Manet, a tall, elegant man-about-town, financially independent, and very much the gentleman artist.

Manet's daring and original technique quickly captured the attention and admiration of the younger artists who were attracted by his new conception of beauty—the charm of everyday reality done in a painterlike manner and with a luminous palette. He painted whatever was pleasing to his eye in his beloved Paris—the races, the well-dressed men and women, the cafés and the theaters, all that he revered of that age of elegance and leisure. In all stages of his career he was attacked bitterly and savagely by the Academicians who blocked official recognition for many years. In his later years he created a fusion between Realism and Impressionism when the problem of luminosity absorbed him and he substituted color for tone and details until his figures became big areas of luminous color against contrasting backgrounds. But all through his life he revealed to the artists of his day an exciting new world to explore and record.

Manet was born in Paris in 1832, the son of well-to-do bourgeoisie who wanted him to study law. He chose to go to sea until they changed their minds. Later, he entered the studio of Couture, where in spite of dissensions with the master, he remained for five years. From that time onward his career was stormy and spectacular. Official juries rejected his works. His paintings *Le Dejeuner sur l'Herbe* and *Olympia* caused scandals. This lack of public appreciation continued for years. In 1881 he was accepted in the Salon, but by that time his health began to give way. He died in Paris in 1883 from gangrene which set in after a leg amputation.

If Manet had devoted his major efforts to etching, he would have become one of the greatest etchers of all time. He worked with great freedom and spontaneity, with vigorous strokes, and rich blacks and intense whites. He made *The Gypsies* when he was only twenty, but his remarkable handling of light and the restless interplay of small short hatchings in the figures and parallel slashes of the background show his complete mastery of a difficult medium. Although his figures are represented in a comparatively static attitude, the print is imbued with movement and vitality.

JAMES ABBOTT McNEILL WHISTLER

The Beggars

HE DREW AN impudent little butterfly on each work of art, and that fluttering signature was the perfect symbol for the many-sided personality known as Jimmy Whistler. He was a great artist, a man-of-letters, a noted wit, and a tireless *bon vivant*. He was also a pugnacious little dandy who cultivated the art of insult and used it with devastating effect on friend and foe alike. Even Oscar Wilde came out second best in their verbal encounters. His verve, his buoyancy, and his flair for the unexpected were typically American, yet he was considered a Frenchman, an Englishman, a Spaniard, and a Japanese, insofar as his art was concerned. Not until long after his death was he considered an American—which he always was.

Whistler was born in Lowell, Massachusetts, in 1834. In 1842 he went with his family to Russia where his father contracted to construct a railroad for the Czar. They were there for seven years until Major Whistler died from the effects of cholera. His widow took the two brothers back to Connecticut until James was ready to enter West Point. He did not distinguish himself at the Military Academy. His love for drawing overshadowed his other studies and he was "invited" to leave. He then joined the Coastal Survey where he learned to etch while preparing government maps and plans. In six months he resigned and went to Paris to continue his art education. He never returned to America.

La vie Bohème was very much to his liking. He must have worked as hard as he frolicked because his work soon impressed some of the best French artists of the time. His posings, epigrams, verbal battles, and rare infectiousness made him a popular legend. He was a gadfly who kept his world in constant ferment and became the most notorious artist of the time. He remained an American in spite of his lifetime expatriation. He was a prophet and an inspiration to such rising Americans as Marin, John Sloan, Boardman Robinson, and others. He served as a bridge from Europe to America and was the progenitor of the American art that followed.

Whistler is considered one of the greatest etchers of all time, and he worked in a period of great etchers. It was claimed his etchings were greater than Rembrandt's. It is a curious note that both masters were concerned with the same subject—beggars. Whistler did several versions of this same print, but the last state remains unsurpassed in quality and artistry. His lines are hard, dry and meaningful—bathed with color that ties all of the graphic elements together with expressive tone and calligraphic astuteness. It is this print about which he remarked: "That may do to stand with the Rembrandts, eh?"

When he died in London in 1903, extra police were assigned to hold back the crowds. But there were no crowds. He was no longer a front-page figure. Even the American Embassy failed to send a representative.

METROPOLITAN MUSEUM OF ART

HILAIRE GERMAIN EDGAR DEGAS

Sortie du Bain

PARIS HAS ALWAYS been fortunate in her brilliant chroniclers. All through her history, artists have been violently in love with her many-faceted aspects and have projected them in terms of their own genius. But perhaps her most dour lover was Edgar Degas, a bitter, withdrawn, and caustic man who distilled the entire life of the city into a series of unforgettable and vivid images. He was a man of means, free to explore and experiment. For a time he became part of the Impressionist movement, but his complex artistic personality set him apart. He was essentially a Classicist, for painting was to him a language of the mind used to create harmonious and ordered images. He was also a Romantic, intrigued by the unusual emotive fragment, the accidental pose, the fleeting movement. He studied and was influenced by Japanese prints and absorbed from them the cool, fragile flatness, the qualities of two-dimensional pattern that one finds in most of his work. Occupational gestures fascinated him, and he spent most of his time sketching circus girls, ballet dancers, actresses and nude women at their toilet. He recorded the social pageantry of his day but was never part of it. He was also a master etcher whose knowledge of technique was prodigious. He used the medium seriously as a major means of expression, and not, as some of his contemporaries did, merely to transpose their work from one medium to another.

The son of a French banker and a Creole mother from New Orleans, Degas was born in Paris in 1834. He was first educated for law, but at the age of twenty-one entered the École des Beaux Arts. A year later he went to Italy, and then returned two years later to Paris and painted historical pictures in the Classical academic tradition. He exhibited at the Salons and led the life of a wealthy man-about-town. After the Franco-Prussian War, in which he took an active part, he associated with the Impressionists and exhibited with them. But gradually his relations with them became more and more strained. In 1886 he ceased to exhibit anywhere and became a recluse. He never married. He worked incessantly in his studio in Paris until his death in 1917.

The striking etching *Sortie du Bain* (Coming Out of the Bath) is a splendid example of dramatic posing and ingenious design. All non-essentials have been ruthlessly eliminated. The moving figure is placed in an envelope of light, and the mass and movement of the body are given character, though little definite form is discernible. The decorative two-dimensional effect of the background is a superb backdrop for his figures. The unusual angle of view is a result of his study of the new art of photography in which the camera transfixes an angle of vision that is not always given to the human eye. The etching may be a bit melodramatic in conception, but it is a graphic summation of all that is best in Degas' art.

63

PAUL CÉZANNE

The Bathers

VENERATED, EMULATED AND quoted by generations after his death, it is an ironic fact that this greatest of modern masters was subjected to savage attacks, shameful calumny, and smug misunderstanding by the public, critics and art officials during his lifetime. A less self-confident and dedicated man would have collapsed in the face of the relentless opposition from even his closest friends and associates. But this unhappy and withdrawn man persisted in his lifelong search for that elusive quality termed "form." More than any other painter, he added new dimensions to Western art. But he died unappreciated and unacknowledged.

Cézanne was born in 1839 in Aix-en-Provence, the son of a wealthy hat manufacturer who later became a banker. For a time he studied law and then, in 1863, to his father's dismay, he decided to follow his real talents and became a painter. He went to Paris and drifted through several art schools. Although he participated in the controversies of the day and was for a time part of that small band of free-thinking artists who were destined to found the Impressionist school, he was essentially a solitary being who distrusted and was uneasy in the gay give-and-take of the artists' groups. He was determined to secure official acceptance and respectability, and each year submitted his paintings to the Salon. Each year they were refused. Finally, in 1882, the judges accepted a portrait. His theories were derided and his work called crude and ugly. Only the Impressionist Exhibitions and the Salon des Indépendants exhibited his work. The dealer Vollard took an interest in him and sold a few paintings. In 1905, a year before his death, a whole room was devoted to his work at the Salon d'Automne. Marriage in 1886 to a model gave him further unhappiness and frustrations. His lack of recognition drove him more and more into himself, a tragic figure beset by doubts and fears. He died in 1906, unaware that he was destined to be accepted as one of the great masters of art.

From Ingres to Matisse there was hardly a famous French painter who did not experiment with the lithographic process at one time or another. The few lithographs created by Cézanne were probably made in the studio of the popular printer Clot. *The Bathers* is but one of a long series of paintings, drawings and studies of nudes known collectively as *Bathers*. The awkwardly posed figures reflect his terror of models. He used drawings which he made in life classes years before and perhaps a small, articulated lay figure for his studies for this great print. The arched trees and the figures all play their part in the rhythmic music of the three-dimensional design; each form is vitally and creatively connected with every other part. In his figure studies Cézanne attempted to rival the Renaissance and Baroque masters in Classical arrangement. He succeeded in creating a masterpiece of monumental form.

64

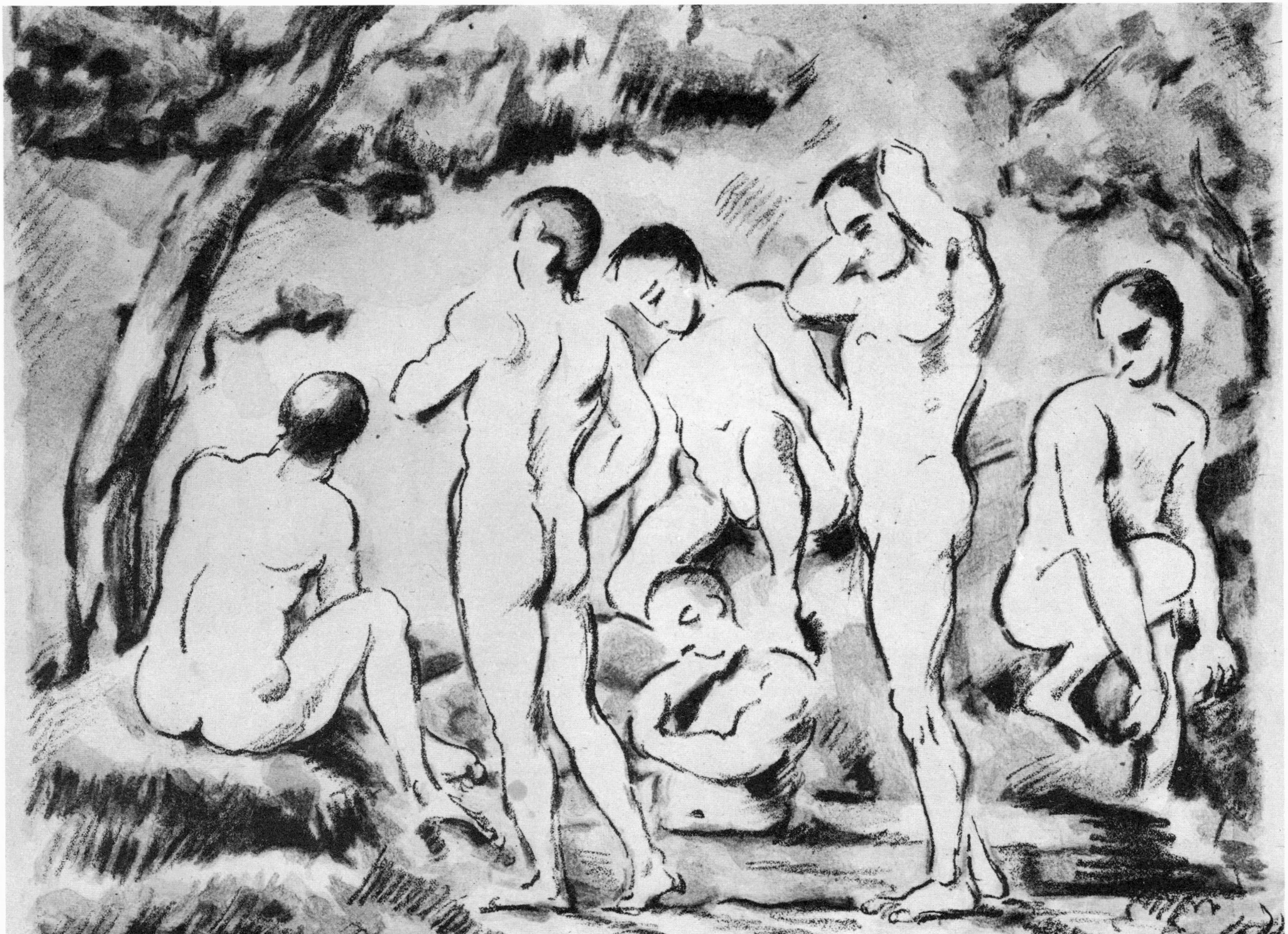

KLEEMAN GALLERY

NATIONAL GALLERY OF ART

ODILON REDON

La Mort

IN J. K. HUYSMANS' curious novel *A Rebours,* the decadent hero of the book, Des Essientes, describes the works of Redon that decorated his walls: "They passed all bounds, transgressing in a thousand ways the established laws of pictorial art, utterly fantastic and revolutionary, the work of a mad and morbid genius." This exotic description is a bit overdrawn, but it does convey the atmosphere generated by the brooding and macabre art of this great solitary artist. He was a gentle man, a thinker, erudite and refined, steeped in the writings of Baudelaire, Flaubert, Poe, and the literature of the Orient. The fantasies bred by his omnivorous reading were translated into a weird symbolical vocabulary of fantastic designs, infinite space, and strangely palpable chimeras. He surrounded his enigmatic creatures with nebulous darkness or luminous air, the very "stuff that dreams are made on."

Redon narrowly missed being born an American. His French father had emigrated to New Orleans during the Napoleonic wars, amassed a comfortable fortune, and married a Creole woman who bore him one child in America. When she was pregnant again, they moved to Bordeaux where, in 1840, Odilon was born. He was a delicate child, introspective and studious. At an early age he was passionately interested in botany, literature and philosophy. When he was twenty he went to Paris to study art with Gérôme. Later he studied etching with Bresdin and lithography with Fantin-Latour. He found the lithographic process the ideal medium to express his mystic visions. He became a master at producing the almost unlimited gamut of black-and-white tones the stone is capable of printing. Active fighting in the Franco-Prussian War added more nightmarish material to an already overwrought mind. In 1879 he married an admirer of his work, and his marriage turned out to be a rare, enduring companionship. After many years of graphic creation he turned to an old love—botany—and created some of the most exquisite flower paintings in French art. Connoisseurs eagerly bought these paintings, and their support enabled him to live comfortably until his death in 1916.

La Mort was inspired by Flaubert's *Temptation of St. Anthony.* It contains some of Redon's favorite symbology. The draped semi-nude figure has the same fumelike whirling gyroscopic spiral that he used in other prints. It leads from the base of the figure upward, ending in a veil-like band of color sheathing the shoulders and partially hidden head. The sprig of flowers above the head may represent the eternalness of art, for he often symbolized art by a flower.

67

PIERRE AUGUSTE RENOIR

La Danse dans la Campagne

RENOIR WAS THE most charming of the great artists of the nineteenth century. He reflects the very essence of the enchantment of French art in his flair for pulsating color, his lyrical expressive line, and his penchant for subject matter that conveys all of the thrills and atmosphere of a Parisian boulevard on a spring day. He was never bound by the numerous theories which were almost epidemic in his day. He painted the subjects which appealed to him as beautiful: nudes, flowers, street scenes, landscapes, young girls, and the homely day-to-day life of his fellow Parisians. He always thought that the beauty of the subject was sufficient to justify the picture. He painted for the sheer pleasure of painting, and, in so doing, managed to sum up in his own way the achievements of not only the Impressionists but the Classicists and the eighteenth-century genre painters as well.

Renoir's roots were as humble as his attitude toward life. The son of a tailor, he was born at Limoges in 1841. At the age of thirteen he started earning his living, first as a china decorator at a porcelain factory, and then as a painter of fans and window blinds. In 1862 he had saved enough money to enable him to study at the studio of Gleyre. Here he met and became friends with Monet, Bazille and Sisley, all of whom played leading parts in the Impressionist movement. In 1880 he married and then traveled extensively in Europe. For the next twenty-five years he resided in Paris during which time his popularity increased and sales zoomed. His style became distinctive, stamped with that aura of voluptuosity that never fell into eroticism. In much of his work he came within a hair's breadth of prettiness, but was saved from it by the sincerity and simplicity of his conception. In later years Renoir feared that the charm and spontaneity of his work were leading him to a dead end. He destroyed paintings and went back to life class where he labored from seven to ten hours a day. He turned more to line and plasticity. The etching *La Danse dans la Campagne* was among the first works denoting his new emphasis on linear composition. At his death in 1919 he was a revered and beloved artist, simple and unassuming in his greatness.

Renoir did not execute many plates. Only twenty-five are catalogued and these were made at the demand of his friends. But he knew and respected the medium and achieved distinctive results in his etchings. *La Danse dans la Campagne* was a version of his painting of the same title, and the subject of a number of drawings. The dancing couple was posed by his brother Edmond Renoir and Suzanne Valadon, a noted artist in her own right and a favorite model of Renoir. The vibrant action is achieved by feathery short lines and a variety of rich textures formed by cross-hatching. In spite of the fact that he worked only in black-and-white, there is an impressive luminosity achieved by his use of velvety blacks and soft grays. It is a charming print that has all of the natural lyrical qualities of his best work and the simplicity of his extremely personal vision.

MARY CASSATT

The Coiffeur

ART IN THE America of the 1860's was a foster child that had to win respectable acceptance. Artists were regarded as strange eccentrics—a race apart. The very thought of a woman aspiring to be a professional artist was unthinkable, especially when the aspiring young woman came from the proper atmosphere of the socially élite of Philadelphia. In spite of parental storms and dire warnings, Mary Cassatt persisted, and, defying conventions, she departed for Europe in 1868—at the age of twenty-three—to study the Old Masters and their methods.

She was captivated by Correggio in Italy, Velasquez in Spain, and Rubens and Hals in the Low Countries. The year 1874 found her established in Paris just in time to participate in the Impressionist movement. The works she saw in the Paris shops by Manet, Degas, Pissarro and Renoir won her by their emancipation of color. In 1877, Degas, who was always to remain a devoted friend and admirer of her work, invited her to exhibit with the Impressionists and she was wholeheartedly accepted by them as an equal *confrère*.

Two influences shaped her work: the exquisite sense of draughtsmanship developed by Degas, and her intensive study of Japanese prints. The first gave her an authoritative and rhythmic line, and the second fashioned her style by the elimination of all superfluous details, consequently giving stress to the essentials. She practiced the various media of printmaking to perfect her draughtsmanship. She developed it so completely that by 1891 she had become one of the outstanding graphic artists of her time. As a woman she was attracted by the relationship of mother and child. With a lack of sentimentality and with real sincerity she became one of the most profound interpreters of this theme. Her other subjects reflected her own charming world of tea parties, evenings at the opera, and her intimate circle of family and friends. The full gamut of her expression and experience can be found in her prints. After a full, rich and creative life, in which she outlived most of her friends and colleagues, she died in France in 1926.

The Coiffeur, a combination of many media—drypoint, aquatint, and softground etching—shows the influence of Japanese prints on her work in the graceful curves of the model and the contrast of her reflection in the mirror with the straight lines of its frame. The broad lines of the chair and the flat patterns of the wallpaper and the rug are typical of the sense of pattern practiced by the Japanese printmakers. Her colors are her own, however, with blues, browns, grays, greens and pink dominating.

MARY CASSATT

In the Omnibus

DEGAS ONCE EXCLAIMED upon seeing a drawing by Mary Cassatt: "I would not have admitted that a woman could draw as well as that." He made this statement when the artist Pissarro submitted some trial proofs of her prints to him for criticism. All of her work is characterized by precision of drawing, honesty of conception and a clear vision which made no compromise with sentimentality and charm.

One of the reasons why looking at a Cassatt print is such a satisfying and relaxing experience is her perfect rapport with her subjects. Her prints are kindly and understanding commentaries on her subjects, gems of observation untainted by personal psychological aberrations. The two women and the plump baby on the seat of the omnibus make for a secure and peaceful scene with the baby resting confidently in her nurse's arm. The serenity of the scene is complete and convincing.

In the Omnibus displays a successful blending of Oriental and Occidental qualities. The arabesque form of the baby's figure, silhouetted against the tan dress of the mother on the left and the brown of the nurse's dress on the right, is a charming color contrast. The bridge viewed within the frame of the bus windows provides another focal point and is a welcome design element of the entire composition. Mary Cassatt's complete works total between one hundred and fifty and two hundred prints. They all attest to the fact that within the range of her sphere of work, she has rarely been surpassed.

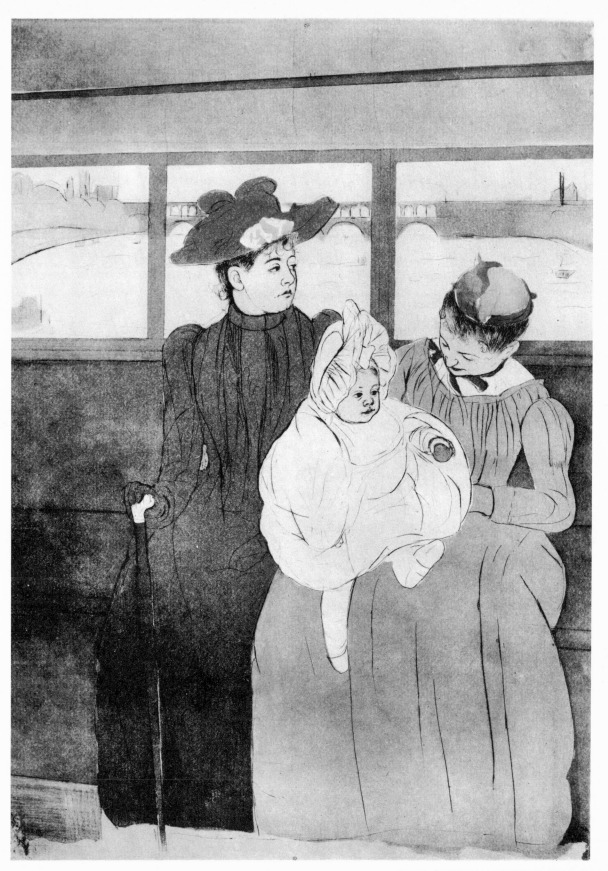

PAUL GAUGUIN

Auti Te Pape

IN RECENT YEARS the life and work of Paul Gauguin have been distorted by a haze of exotic claptrap that has hidden the man and his genuine contributions to art. Stripping aside the romantic wrappings of popularization, one finds Gauguin to have been a tenacious, frank and rather simple-minded man with no developed esthetic or intellectual background. The almost suicidal sacrifices that he made for his painting evolved from his fanatical belief that art could be regenerated by contact with primitive life. He was neither temperamentally nor intellectually equipped for the task. He was primarily a decorator, a magnificent colorist, a fine designer and a master of flowing line. His use of distortion for purely decorative ends has alienated the adherents of the modern architectural doctrine of art, and, in his own time, his non-naturalistic handling of subjects was the antithesis of Impressionist practice. On the other hand, he profoundly influenced the Expressionist movement of our own century by the savage emotive power of his expression.

Gauguin's life is better known than his work. He was born in Paris in 1848. In 1851 he and his family emigrated to Peru where he remained until 1858 when he was sent back to France to be educated. From the age of seventeen to twenty-three he served in the mercantile marine and then joined a firm of Paris stockbrokers. For the next ten years he led the life of a prosperous bourgeois, and then suddenly gave up his job to devote all his time to painting, which until then he had practiced only as a hobby. He was soon without funds and his wife and children left him to rejoin her family in Denmark. In desperation he sold all his pictures at auction and left for Tahiti. Two years later he was back in Paris with more paintings and a Javanese woman. His pictures caused a sensation, but few were sold. Another auction brought enough funds for him to return to Tahiti. He lived there until 1901, and then went to the Marquesas where he died in 1903.

His prints are regarded by many critics as his greatest works of art. Like his paintings, they are the work of a decorator and colorist, but his true affinity was for the black-and-white woodcut. He cut his blocks crudely and powerfully, using hand pressure to get his impressions in any tonal range he wanted. This natural technique produced prints that evolved from the true sculptural nature of the medium and its tools. *Auti Te Pape* (Woman at the River) is a stunning example of his broad and powerful treatment of forms and his instinctive omission of details. The blacks are rich, solid, and heavy. Irregularities of hand pressure created modulations of tone. His distribution of light is dramatic, although it seems loose in design. The woman in the right background is silhouetted in white against black. This double silhouetting is a favorite device of Gauguin.

75

PAUL GAUGUIN

Noa Noa

THE LANDSCAPE AND the subjects Gauguin found in Tahiti and the Marquesas were marvelously suited to an artist who regarded all his pictures as patterns, who approached them as a decorator, and planned even the smallest woodcut as carefully as the greatest mural painting. He went back to the Italian woodcut artists of the second quarter of the sixteenth century to emulate their treatment of forms and their ignoring of decoratively unessential detail.

Noa Noa has a richness of color which only seems possible in black-and-white. Gauguin's practice of applying hand pressure in the printing of the block has resulted in flashes of white that encircle the foreground figure, scratched in lines and half tints that can be seen in the background landscape, and deeply gouged black areas that form the foreground and frame. The entire print is wonderfully decorative and its emotional impact is immediate. It is graphic evidence that his prophecy was fulfilled when he wrote: "I feel sure that the time will come when my woodcuts, so different as they are from all that is now produced, will acquire some value."

JEAN LOUIS FORAIN

The Return of the Prodigal Son

FORAIN HAD THE same admirable faculty of recording the life about him as his *confrères* Daumier, Lautrec and Steinlen. Like them, he sought his subjects on the streets of Paris and pictorialized his intimate knowledge of Parisian life in a distinctive personal style. He was perhaps closest to the humanity of Daumier, who, like himself, contributed his caustic graphic comments to contemporary French journals. For the greater part of his life, Forain contributed his graphic interpretations of French life and mores. He was as prodigal in production as Daumier. He vilified the brutalities of the first World War. His etchings of the Paris law courts are every bit as damning as Daumier's scathing series. He devoutly recorded the miracles of Lourdes, moved to a deep compassion by the drama of faith and religiosity. In all of his work there is almost an obsessive compulsion to bring to the surface the vicissitudes of the common man which he expressed with sincerity, sympathy and compelling graphic power.

Forain's talents were recognized at an early age in Rheims, where he was born in 1852. A local painter persuaded his parents to allow him to study art in Paris. After a few years of preliminary study he entered the atelier of Carpeaux the sculptor. He found that his gifts were for the graphic arts, and he left to do pictorial reporting by sketching the people and their life in the city streets. This basic training laid the foundation for all of the great prints he created up to his death in 1931.

The period in which he etched *The Return of the Prodigal Son* saw him at the height of his powers of graphic exposition and technical performance. His grasp of character was developed with exquisite subtlety. His handling of light and shade showed a direct affinity to the etched art of Rembrandt. There was a strong dramatic force and a realism in his work that showed great power in spite of his economy of line and tone. He usually made many sketches of a single subject and subtracted superfluous elements from each successive version. *The Return of the Prodigal Son* went through several transformations until it reached the direct and simple means employed in rendering the background support of the two central figures. Every line and stroke is important in endowing the simple composition with deep and dramatic meaning.

In the twenty-five years since his death, Forain's reputation has grown and become firmly established. His passion for art, his love for people and his technical ability are all reflected in the many great prints that bear his signature.

VINCENT VAN GOGH

Sorrow

THE POIGNANT STORY of the life of the tormented Van Gogh has been told and retold with varying degrees of accuracy and melodrama. His brief career furnished enough lurid events for a score of legends. All his life he lived in a continuous and consuming frenzy of creative intensity, a suicidal drive that led to some great art, madness and ultimate self-destruction. Like other paranoiacs, he was obsessed with a mission, a zeal to aid struggling humanity, and when he failed to perform it as a lay preacher, he turned to art for his evangelical efforts. Art, however, was more than a needed means of expression; it was also a passionate means of spiritual development. It was only when he came in contact with such artists as Lautrec, Gauguin and Seurat that he became more the artist and less the missionary. Critics still differ in their estimates of his work. Many consider him to be one of our major artists, while others consider him a minor Romantic Realist. But all agree that his last pictures, best organized and most controlled, belong to the body of the world's great art.

Van Gogh was born in Holland in 1853, the son of a Protestant pastor. At the age of sixteen he was employed by a picture dealer at The Hague and later at the branch offices in London and Paris. He left to become a schoolmaster at Ramsgate, and then went back to Holland to train as a minister, but he never completed his training. In 1878 he became a lay preacher working among the Belgian miners, but was dismissed for his fanatical asceticism. He then started to draw and later, in his mid-thirties, went to Paris to live with his brother Theo. His contacts with his great contemporaries made him the artist we know. In 1888 he went to Arles to paint, and then followed a series of deteriorating mental attacks, hospitalizations and periods of custodial care. He continued to paint and was at the very peak of his powers until July of 1890, when he shot himself.

Van Gogh executed a few prints—some etchings and lithographs. His lithograph *Sorrow* is one of his most expressive subjects. It was inspired by a pregnant and despondent streetwalker whom he rescued from cold and hunger and to whom he gave employment as his model. It is somber and powerful, with firm decisive lines tracing a drooping arch around the figure that is the very essence of the emotion conveyed. It transmits an incredibly moving experience, and certainly belongs among the great prints of our time.

80

Sorrow

Vincent

JAMES ENSOR

The Cathedral

FANTASTIC SUBJECT MATTER has been found in European art in all periods. Perhaps this is because throughout the history of civilization the grotesqueries of society have made it difficult for the sensitive and perceptive artist to maintain and express a rational point of view. Examination of all great art will reveal elements of fantasy which is the artist's symbolic and pictorial comment on the phantasmagoria of the human scene around him. The Dutch artist Bosch, working at the end of the Gothic period, transformed traditional fantasy into a personal and original vision and became the predecessor of such artists as Callot, Bruegel, Goya, Klee, and Ensor.

Born in Ostend, Belgium, in 1860, James Ensor was placed by circumstance at the crossroads of two epochs. He matured in the period of post-Impressionism, antedating even Van Gogh's efforts and Gauguin's first successes. He worked well into the twentieth century, a forerunner of Modernism and particularly of Expressionism. He represents the very essence of transition. The two centuries spanned by his lifetime contradict and complement one another. The researches in color of the nineteenth century were based on a belief in the sensory, and the pictorial art of these painters portrayed what met the eye. The anti-Naturalism of the twentieth century emphasized the spirit and produced artists of pure intellect, free imagination—poet-painters. Ensor was the prophet of the unrealistic lyricism of today.

His personal life was unexciting. He studied for a short while at the Brussels Academy of Fine Arts and then returned to his native town. He never again left it. His work attracted the attention of only a few discerning critics and collectors until 1896 when he received recognition from his government. From that time on he received a great deal of attention, particularly from the poet Verhaeren. In 1929 the government bestowed a baronetcy on him, the traditional Belgian recognition of a great artist. According to his own wry estimate, he lived on long past his time. A self-portrait made in 1938 bore the ironic inscription: "This portrait, like its author, is in a state of decay." When he died in 1949, he was mourned as the greatest of modern Belgian artists.

The Cathedral is one of his most profound and bitter works. The etching technique, with its thin, brittle lines, is masterful. The subject was a theme to which he returned again and again. It is symbolic of the attempt to give meaning and dignity to human values which are mocked and destroyed by the mob. In this print the cathedral stands magnificent and monumental, but the fantastic members of the carnival mob turn their backs both to the church and to the military lined up in front of it. It is temporal and spiritual power rising above the disorderly mob. It is typical of his Expressionist works which inspire the beholder to create his own interpretation of meaning in the light of his own background and spirit.

83

ARISTIDE MAILLOL

Nude 1

THE SENSE OF tradition has always been a strong factor in the development of French art. It has endured in spite of successive esthetic revolutions and counter-revolutions. It had been hidden and disguised by bold and brash statements in manifestoes and pronouncements. But it is omnipresent and easily discovered by even the most superficial examination of the art of any period. There are always definite and unmistakable progressions in philosophy and style that lead from one artist to another. Maillol is a traditionalist and his work is an excellent case-in-point to prove the force of tradition on art. A dissection of his art will reveal diverse influences. Each played a part in his growth and helped to establish him as one of the greatest interpreters of the nude in modern art history.

Maillol has been described as "the most serene and instinctively Greek of the moderns," but his pagan devotion to the nude more logically stems from that French libertine tradition that reaches from the Fontainebleau School, through Poussin, Watteau, Fragonard, Ingres, Courbet, Gauguin, Renoir, to Matisse and the Surrealists of today. Essentially he is closest to Ingres in his search for and celebration of the ideal of female beauty. When he undertook lithography, the lush forms and unashamed sensualism of Renoir left their mark on his prints. But in all of his work reverence for the nude and earthiness of conception are distinctly Maillol.

Maillol's forbears were of peasant stock and he was born in 1861 in the region of Banyuls in the Pyrenees. He went to Paris in 1882 to study painting at the École des Beaux Arts. When he first saw some paintings by Gauguin, new horizons in design opened for him, and he incorporated his newly found ideas in woodcutting, tapestry design and lithography. He stopped printmaking abruptly in 1900, and devoted himself completely to sculpture. He became an acclaimed master with work that emulated the grace and serenity of the Greek. He returned to printmaking after a decade's abstention and worked on woodcut illustrations for many of the masterpieces of fine bookmaking published by Vollard. Up until his death in 1944 he concentrated on drawings and prints of the female nude.

The lithograph *Nude 1,* a standing figure viewed from the rear, demonstrates his genius for expressing form in outline and mass. Every calligraphic nuance in the drawing attests to the lyrical accent of his line, the subtle transition of planes and his rare ability to transmute lithographic textures into living and glowing flesh. In later life Maillol developed a great enthusiasm for Egyptian sculpture. He admired its air of calm and permanence. This nude reflects that admiration in the feeling of arrested motion, a poised stillness that is as poignant in conception as the Egyptian masterpieces he studied. It projects, as does all of his work, a sense of humaneness and a spirituality that always inspire a profound response.

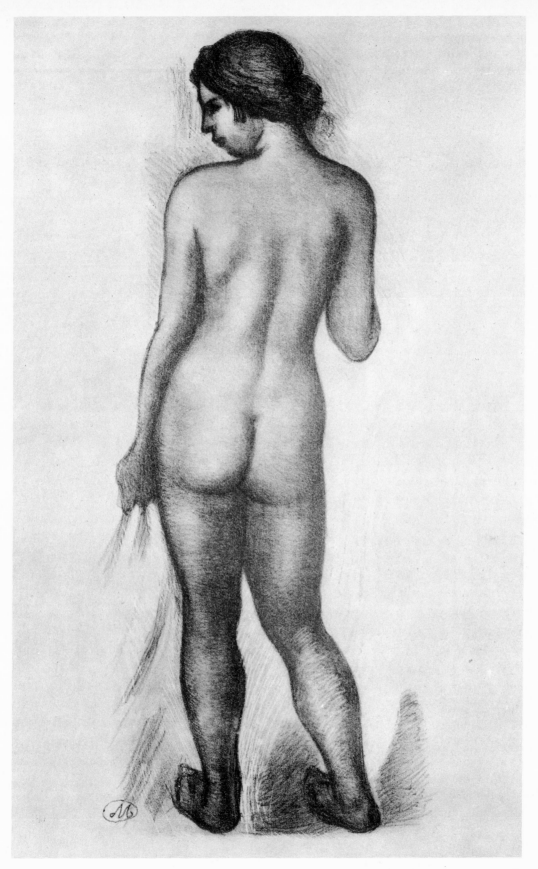

NATIONAL GALLERY OF ART

NATIONAL GALLERY OF ART

ARISTIDE MAILLOL

Nude 2

A CRITIC ONCE wrote of Maillol's classic line: "His lyrical lines have an innate grace, they vibrate and sing, they are at once naïve and suave, chaste and sensual." Although his nudes stem from the charming and piquant tradition of Boucher, Watteau and Fragonard, his studies of the work of Gauguin, the classic Greek sculpture and the sculpture of ancient Egypt, have given his nudes a monumental character, a stillness of grace and a felicity of immobility that his more frivolous forbears would have deplored.

Nude 2 is a classic pose designed to create rhythmic interplay between curvilinear lines and the textures created by his flesh tones. The face is barely realized, an enigmatic and anonymous countenance that is merely a convention and not a likeness. The raised knee, the bent elbow and the inclined head are realized in one graceful sweeping outline encircling the entire figure. He has expressed the poetry of the female figure in a few sweeping lines, lines that have grace and beauty and have served to model one of the great nude studies in the art of printmaking.

EDVARD MUNCH

The Cry

DURING THE FIRST decade of this century, an art movement was born in Germany that profoundly influenced all contemporary art. It began because the younger German artists had too long been forced into the mold of German nineteenth-century Classicism and Romanticism. They organized a series of secessions and revolts in protest against this regimentation which finally resolved into a single movement named Expressionism.

The dominant forces in art were those of the School of Paris, whose artists were occupied with the problems of post-Impressionism. The new movement filled them with horror. They abhorred the introspection, soul-searching, mystic contemplation and philosophical speculation of this *Neue Kunst*. The Expressionists borrowed some of the post-Impressionist vocabulary of design and plastic organization, but as the emotional concepts of the Expressionists became more intense, their need for other means of expression increased and they had to look elsewhere for their material. They went to the schools of the "savages" and utilized the art of distortion so brilliantly exemplified in Negro sculptures and the neolithic arts. The immediate father of this German revolution in art was not a German, but a Norwegian, Edvard Munch.

Munch was born in southern Norway in 1863. When seventeen, he entered the State School of Art. Two years later he set up his studio and became involved in the intellectual life of the time. By the end of 1880, Munch was recognized by his colleagues as the most original and important artist among them. In 1889 he received a government stipend to study art in Paris. In Paris he did not follow the paths of Impressionism for long, but preserved his Northern introspective direction. In 1892 he left Paris for Berlin and remained there to establish and lead the formative groups of German artists who were seeking direction. His path led ultimately to Expressionism, and he was hailed as the new master of Northern art who revealed his expression through inwardly conceived images and purely emotional stimuli. His best work was done before 1910, and from that year until his death in 1944, he was mainly occupied with pictorial problems of painting.

Printmaking became a most important part of his work as early as 1894. He worked in every medium and exploited the special potentialities of each medium, repeating again and again subjects he had already painted. Lithography proved especially attractive with its opportunities for broad handling. He demonstrated his affinity for the medium in the amazing lithograph *The Cry*. Its pattern of swirling, vibrating curves and diagonals almost make audible the sense of drama visible in the frightened face of the woman. The powerful, pulsating lines portray with great graphic force the unseen forces that can fill a human being with fear and anxiety. It is one of the most terrifying and expressive prints ever created.

NATIONAL GALLERY OF ART

HENRI DE TOULOUSE-LAUTREC

Guy et Mealy dans Paris qui Marche

THE STORY OF Henri de Toulouse-Lautrec is almost legend by now. Of all the many colorful personalities of his place and period, he alone symbolizes, and is identified with, the shifting kaleidoscope and social whirl of Paris during the gay nineties. Although he was dwarfed and deformed by a series of childhood accidents, Lautrec entered the feverish night life of Paris with great eagerness. His diminutive figure was seen everywhere. Pencil and sketch-pad in hand, he recorded the posturings of the "girls," the gestures and movements of the theater, its actors and audiences, and the singers and dancers of Parisian café society. He knew, and became known by, every famous and infamous celebrity, and they in turn became the *dramatis personae* of countless paintings, sketches, posters and prints.

He was born a delicate and rachitic child in Albi in southern France on November 24, 1864. His father was Count Alphonse de Toulouse-Lautrec, head of one of the oldest aristocratic French families, which traced its ancestry back to the ninth century. Several bad falls left his legs grotesquely stunted while his torso developed normally. He was doomed to a life of comparative physical inactivity, much to the disappointment of his sports-worshipping father. Only through his art did he express his desires and admiration for an active life. After a few years of academic training, he established himself as an artist in Montmartre with the help of a family allowance. From that time on, Lautrec gave us some of the greatest works of art that the School of Paris has ever created.

Of all the sections of the mad whirl of gaslit Paris that he portrayed, the theaters, cabarets and music halls were the greatest magnets and inspiration for his graphic powers. Perhaps it was because he worshipped physical beauty, or that the animated, elegant personalities became dazzling symbols of the intoxicating gaiety which he constantly sought. Much of his greatest work consists of portrayals of characters in the entertainment world. The actors Guy and Mealy, popular favorites of the period, are shown in a scene from one of their successful plays. These are not literal portraits, but an expert molding into types. The two figures are in their very essence theatrical—the sum total of innumerable observations. Lautrec once said to Yvette Guilbert: "I don't detail you, I totalize you." That is exactly what he did in this dynamic lithograph.

Lautrec died two months before his thirty-seventh birthday, a victim of his own obsessive dissipations. It is as a result of his genius that many of his subjects have lived long beyond their talents and their songs. He was merciless in his portrayals, but his cruelest caricatures were of himself.

HENRI DE TOULOUSE-LAUTREC

La Grande Loge

THE GAIETY AND feverish excitement of Paris at play—her clowns, actors, comedians. dancers, singers, and the elegant parade of fashionables who were their patrons—have all become synonymous with the art of Toulouse-Lautrec. He strolled with them and among them and sketched them with a merciless and unerring eye. He pinned their dazzling forms to his paper with a refreshing lack of moralizing, for, just as were his subjects, so was he a habitué of their world and very much part of its aimless pleasure-seeking. Lautrec the hedonist became Lautrec the objective reporter when he was before his easel. He created one brilliant and all-embracing silhouette into which all of his *dramatis personae* were dissolved. He eliminated details of the people he portrayed and created a general abstraction, an entity which embodied the essence of the personality he dissected and was as readily recognizable as is the most literal portrait.

La Grande Loge is a fine example of his graphic shorthand. The two women are types, not individuals, and the gentleman in the left background, with his top hat making a striking contrast to the light textures and tonalities of the background, is simply one of Lautrec's rather dissipated men-about-town. The setting of a theater box was a favorite with artists of the nineties. Degas and Mary Cassatt among others used this set for several subjects. The light hat and dark coat of the woman on the left, and the dark hat and light coat of the woman on the right keep the eyes traveling in a carefully planned circuit that touches each focal point in turn. It is a magnificent and expressive Lautrec production.

ART INSTITUTE OF CHICAGO

KAETHE KOLLWITZ

Self-Portrait

IF ANY PORTRAIT can be a visual summation of a long and creative life, then surely this serene self-portrayal, done by the artist when she was seventy-five, is a forceful and penetrating graphic autobiography. The chapters are all there; the weary droop of the shoulder, the dignity and resignation of the handsome, aged face and the tired lines of the mouth symbolize an entire lifetime dedicated to depicting with great tenderness and mastery the tragedies, the struggles and the sufferings of the common people.

Kaethe Kollwitz was born on July 8, 1867, in Koenigsberg, East Prussia. Her father, Karl Schmidt, was almost a stereotype of the crusading European free-thinker. Just as he was about to take his bar examinations, he decided that his views would not jibe with those of the guardians of Germanic jurisprudence. He therefore became an expert mason, and then succeeded his own father-in-law as leader and pastor of the Free Religious Congregation, a creed that somewhat resembles the Unitarians and Congregationalists of our own country. From her forbears Kaethe Kollwitz inherited the fervent religious feelings, the habit of philosophical speculation and the patterns of revolutionary thinking that characterized her life and art from early girlhood until her death at the age of seventy-eight.

In 1891 she married Dr. Karl Kollwitz who established a medical clinic in the workingmen's quarter of Berlin. Both dedicated themselves to social service. This consecration served to furnish the substance and inspiration for all her subsequent work. It was at the clinic that she came into direct contact with the suffering and aspiring humanity which she transmuted by her art into social comment, rich in creative expression, human symbolism and graphic form.

For more than four decades she created great prints. Her monumental print cycles—*The Weavers, Peasant War, War* and *Death*—were hailed as art events of the first magnitude. She became the first woman ever to be elected to the Berlin Academy of Art. The rise of Hitler and the Nazis provided the material for her greatest print sequence, *Death*. Although she had an opportunity to leave Germany when the Nazis came to power, she courageously remained with the people she loved and had always championed.

In 1936 her husband died, and for the last three years of her life she lived at Moritzburg Castle as a guest of the Prince of Saxony. Those who saw her just before her death had the feeling that she was living in a serene inner world. This is the mood and feeling that this last *Self-Portrait* conveys. It seems to reflect a premonition of death and a withdrawal into a brighter world to await it. It is one of the most eloquent self-portraits in the history of art, and a monument of great printmaking art.

95

KAETHE KOLLWITZ

Frauenkopf

KAETHE KOLLWITZ HAD the rare facility of investing every subject she created with her own vast humanity, her compassionate sincerity and a complete and unswerving honesty of expression. Her portraits of the working men and women of Germany were not literal portrayals, but splendid archetypes that embodied and symbolized the ravages and scars that hard toil, starvation and disease leave on the human form and face. Her figures are dramatic in pose and attitude, not for the sake of drama or theatrics, but to emphasize and underline her meaning—for she was an artist with a message, a message and a sermon in every print. Like her great predecessors Goya, Daumier and Forain, she created and evaluated a unique microcosm peopled with the oppressed and downtrodden, and she could only offer them her great compassion.

Her etching portrait *Frauenkopf* (Head of Woman) is probably a graphic summation of all the faces of all work-worn women. Each bitten line is needed for this perceptive portrayal. There are no unessential elements added for the sake of technique. The technique is subservient to conception and expression. It is a face you will see on any farm and in any factory. It is a face with history graven into each feature.

96

BUCHHOLZ GALLERY

PIERRE BONNARD

Le Bain

FOR MORE THAN sixty years, Pierre Bonnard was the living embodiment of all that was charming and felicitous in the art of the School of Paris. In his long life he explored the most diverse territories in art. He painted the casual world around him. Flower-filled rooms, gardens, the Paris boulevards, and, above all, women were his favorite subjects. His exquisite studies of women used their forms as decorative segments of a charming whole with little attempt to transcribe their personal loveliness. He has been called the enchanter, the painter of marvels and the magician. Whatever the subject or genre, he always expressed himself with ease, charm and conviction.

He was born in 1867 in a lovely Paris suburb, the son of well-to-do parents who raised him in the typically cloudless and uneventful milieu of a bourgeois youth. His father arranged for him to study law which he did in the mornings, but he gave his afternoons entirely to art. He sketched in the Latin Quarter and painted and drew at the Académie Julian and later at the École des Beaux Arts. In 1889 he failed his Law Orals, but sold a design for a champagne poster. His father reluctantly consented to allow him to be a full-time artist.

It was a fertile period for any young artist. The Impressionists had opened new roads to boldness which the younger generation were busily sidetracking for even more daring and freer vistas. Bonnard played his full role in this exciting reconquest. It is impossible to analyze in a few paragraphs the evolution of so complex and renewable an artist. He once said: "My first pictures were done by instinct, the others with more method perhaps. Instinct which nourishes method can often be superior to a method which nourishes instinct." Bonnard attained mastery when he was twenty-five and maintained it gloriously until his death in 1947 when he was nearly eighty.

Bonnard was truly one of the great masters of the lithograph and he created a mass of graphic art to bear out this estimate. He started creating his first stones at the same time as Lautrec. Both these artists were encouraged and supported by the amazing publisher Vollard, who also commissioned Bonnard to provide illustrations for several classics. Bonnard's lithographs for *Daphnis and Chloe* made it perhaps the most beautifully illustrated book since the eighteenth century.

The figure study *Le Bain* is a later lithograph and one of the finest in his long series of nudes. As in all his other studies of women, there is no attempt at individual characterization. She is merely a lovely and pleasing segment of a charming design that encompasses the vari-textured tiles behind the figure, the strong horizontal of the tub rim and the lovely sloping lines of the model's body. The modeling of the body is strong and sure, with textural areas creating a truly plastic conception of the figure.

99

HENRI MATISSE

Seated Odalisque

Henri matisse is considered by many critics as one of the two greatest painters of his age. For almost fifty years he explored the problems of plastic form and color. His significance and the extent of his influence are equaled in modern times only by Picasso. He was one of modern art's greatest theorists, and his comments exerted a potent and lasting influence. In the frenetic and shifting history of modern art movements, his own philosophy seemed serene and simple: "What I dream of is an art that is equilibrated, pure and calm, free of any disturbing subject matter." With the exception of an occasional experiment in a new style or technique, Matisse kept to the tranquil tenets of his esthetic. He found the motifs of his art close to home—his studio, scenes from his window, and his models. But each time he repeated these subjects, he did so with new daring and plastic variations.

Matisse's long lifetime (1869–1954) spanned a great deal of art history. It ranged from Impressionism to Fauvism, and from Cubism to Abstractionism and the other "isms" of our day. He was born in the north of France, and after a brief career as a law clerk, he turned to art and studied with Bougereau and then with Gustave Moreau. Official recognition came late in his career. In 1921 the Luxembourg Museum purchased one of his *Odalisques*. He exhibited with the Fauves, but was never a convinced member of that violent group. The greatest influence on his art was the art of the Mohammedan Orient. He found his true expression in the flat decorative color surfaces, the stylization of objects, the dominance of color over form and the contrasting of ornamental surfaces. Matisse never imitated Oriental art, but adopted its principles of decoration for his own expression. His series of draped and semi-draped nudes, the *Odalisques,* brilliantly reflect the lush ornateness, the play of decorative line and the concentration on pattern.

In his lithograph *Seated Odalisque,* much emphasis is placed on the patterns of the background wall, the fabric design on the sofa and the diaphanous skirt of the subject. But so faithful was his eye to the essential form of the original that he could allow his decorative sense full play without betraying his subject. His own words best illustrate his approach to his subject: "Suppose I want to paint the body of a woman. First of all I endow it with grace and charm, but I know that something more than that is necessary. I try to condense the meaning of this body by drawing the essential lines. The charm will then become less apparent at first glance, but in the long run it will begin to emanate from the new image. This image at the same time will be enriched by a wider meaning, a more comprehensively human one, while the charm, being less apparent, will not be its only characteristic, it will be merely one element in the general conception of the figure."

BUCHHOLZ GALLERY

BUCHHOLZ GALLERY

HENRI MATISSE

Odalisque

FROM THE RENAISSANCE to the present day, from Cranach to Matisse, the female form has always served as one of the most challenging subjects for the world's greatest artists. One can cut across art history to reveal the development of this theme which has been of paramount importance in all periods.

The Greeks invented the nude as an idea and an ideal, and the early Christian artists used nudity as a symbol of our continuous and lasting fall from grace. Gothic art used the nude figure so that heights of virtuosity could be displayed on a fold in the skin, or a bulge of a muscle. The nude came to its finest flowering in Venice where Titian, Tintoretto and others magnificently exalted woman and painted her resplendent, regal and divine in her nakedness. With Ingres we come to the modern battle between sensuality and style, with style winning and demanding a line rigidly controlled by the intellect as in Cézanne and Manet, and losing to emotion in the nudes of Gauguin and Renoir.

Matisse's highly modeled nudes and semi-nudes stem more from an Oriental tradition of decoration than from the Western progression of the nude as an entity and a symbol. It was not the female body *per se* that occupied the expression of Matisse, but the interplay of the lines of the body with the surrounding background motifs. In the lithograph *Odalisque,* it is the counterpoint of calligraphy in the beads, the diaphanous robe, the ring, the slope of the shoulders, the spiral of the thighs, the droop of the breast and the arch of the hand that create a vibrant and rhythmic study. The flat line of the lithograph crayon was singularly appropriate for his modeling in depth. *Odalisque* is a fitting masterpiece in the long tradition of the female figure in art.

103

JOHN MARIN

Brooklyn Bridge

THE FIRST DECADE of this century was a tumultuous one for the arts in America. Provocative theories on art, formulated by the young Modernists of the School of Paris, were a magnet that drew many of our own painters to the Seine. In the cafés and ateliers there was great talk of Seurat, Cézanne and the new Cubism of Picasso; and, more important, the work of these artists could be seen and analyzed in the many galleries. When our expatriates returned home, heady with all they had seen, they made the subject of art intoxicating for those who had stayed at home. Art became a vital part of the American scene, and the exciting new art was soon to be seen in the little gallery of the photographer Alfred Stieglitz.

Stieglitz met John Marin in Paris, admired his work, and began an association that lasted nearly forty years. Marin was the perfect portrait of an American Yankee— lean, laconic, fiercely independent and completely honest. He took to art rather late in life, when he was twenty-nine. He was born in New Jersey in 1870, received his education there, and was unhappy at a series of jobs. Art interested him and he studied for several years at the Pennsylvania Academy and the Art Students League. He left for Paris at the age of thirty-five. In Paris he took to etching to support himself. The revival of etching which Whistler stimulated was still in force and he sold many etched plates of Parisian scenes. He became creatively interested in the medium and developed a style that was unique. When his style became too modernistic to interest the conservative dealers who purchased his work, he turned to watercolors, a medium that he could wander about in as he pleased, satisfying only himself. Fellow artists became enthusiastic about his work and brought it to the attention of Stieglitz who exhibited his first group in 1909. In 1911 Marin returned home permanently and was caught up in the excitement and activity that centered in Stieglitz's gallery. He continued etching, particularly New York scenes, and ranged the Eastern seaboard for subjects that he immortalized in watercolors. His great gift for drawing, developed from his etching, is reflected in all his paintings. He formulated a graphic shorthand that summarized the very essence of his subjects—calligraphic notations derived from rectangles, cones, zigzags and squares. Marin died in 1953, a great American artist who fully realized his gifts.

The subject of the etching *Brooklyn Bridge* is one that he explored many times in various media. He quickly responded to the fierce power of urban life which was symbolized to him by bridges and skyscrapers. This particular etching is a splendid example of his mature structural style. He has abstracted the structure in zigzag planes, toppling verticals and expressionist whirls, playing circular motifs against solid masses with magnificent sureness. It is an overwhelming impression of strength and bigness, the very essence of urban vitality.

Marin 17
Brooklyn Bridge

John Marin

METROPOLITAN MUSEUM OF ART

GEORGES ROUAULT

Crucifixion

GEORGES ROUAULT WAS born amidst exploding shells during the bombardment of Paris by the Versaillais of the Commune in May of 1871. The shellfire forced his mother to take refuge in the cellar of her house and it hastened the labor and birth of the child. Perhaps the furor of his natal day was to presage the turbulence and fervor of much of his later work, for in all of it there is the seething of a barely repressed violence—his reaction to brutality, ugliness and crime. He has put this forceful condemnation of contemporary evil into a series of such dynamic and forceful prints, that the grandeur, strength and passion of his indictments have produced a body of great religious art.

His childhood flowered under the affectionate eye and guidance of his grandfather, a print lover who admired and collected the prints of Daumier, Callot and Rembrandt. Rouault's very early familiarity with the work of Daumier in particular influenced the conception of much of his later graphic art. Daumier's deep and sincere humanity hiding just behind the façade of a savage bitterness is an element that fashioned Rouault's personal vision and emotional conviction. His early training as a stained-glass maker may account for his technique of juxtaposing glowing reds, greens and blues, and his use of heavy black outlines so reminiscent of the glassmaker's use of heavily leaded contours.

Rouault's formal art training began in the studio of Gustave Moreau where he quickly became Moreau's favorite pupil. Moreau was a Medievalist who was devoted to moral sentiments and opposed to superficial reality in art. These were tenets that Rouault eagerly embraced. His own subsequent philosophy was shaped by the writings and personal friendship of Léon Bloy, the noted Catholic writer, and thereafter the most dominant theme in the work of Rouault is the one of sin and redemption.

Most of his notable work has been done as a printmaker. He uses the etching and aquatint media for the most part. His impressive color plates for *La Passion* and *Le Cirque* series, and the powerful black-and-white plates for his most memorable series, the *Miserère et Guerre,* definitely establish him as one of the most important printmakers of all time. The plate *Crucifixion* is a comparatively recent engraving, and is typical of his distinctive style. All of the figures are non-realistic. Heavy black lines outline the faces and forms, and they are almost abstract in their function. This print is saturated with the artist's emotional intensity, expressing his religious feelings directly through the image of the Son of God. There are almost no details. It is rather the extreme simplicity of his forms that convey Rouault's emotional participation in the tragic event. It is this fine simplicity—his revolt against a sophisticated art and world—that is the very root of his genius.

JACQUES VILLON

Les Haleurs

IN THE EARLY part of this century a new manner of painting was developed by a group of French artists. At their very first exhibition, the much impressed Matisse bestowed the title Cubism on the style because of its geometrical construction. It was Braque, Picasso and a few others who established the fundamental idea of Cubism which was to dissociate the planes of a seen object and to rearrange them in a picture, so organized that they would give a truer emotional or structural sense than the original "appearance." From its inception, Villon became one of Cubism's pioneers, and he is now the oldest of the original group, and the only remaining artist who is still maintaining its discipline.

He was born as Gaston Duchamp in 1875. He adopted the name Jacques Villon after he left his father's law office, a promising young attorney who preferred to become an artist. The tradition was strong in his family. His grandfather was a painter and an engraver, and both brothers and his sister became distinguished artists. It was a great many years before recognition and support were given to Villon, and in the interim he was forced to earn his livelihood by several activities. He became a draughtsman for a French comic paper and later an engraver. He was and is one of the most proficient engravers of all time—both for his magnificent original etchings and engravings, and for his color etching reproductions after pictures by such artists as Matisse, Picasso and others. These color etching reproductions are among the most amazing technical performances in the history of the medium, and rival the great plates of the eighteenth-century French engravers who left us stunning color engravings of the paintings of their own day. Since 1930 Villon has issued three or four original prints each year. They all exhibit his amazing technique and his strict adherence to the tenets of Cubism.

Les Haleurs takes us back to one of the sources of Cubism—Italian painting. The early Italian painters were all composers of space relation, an underlying principle of Cubism. The dynamics of this etching may have its genesis in the thrusts and movements of Uccello. The straining nude figures are placed on a diagonal plane and broken into thousands of geometrically precise segments. The entire plate is honeycombed with criss-crossed and cross-hatched lines, relieved only by small areas of tone. This shimmering network of lines keeps the composition in constant movement and makes the linear action a living force in Villon's conception. Only an artist of great technical dexterity could control and unify such a complex linear pattern. Villon has done so with no sense of confusion, and with splendid control of all the graphic elements.

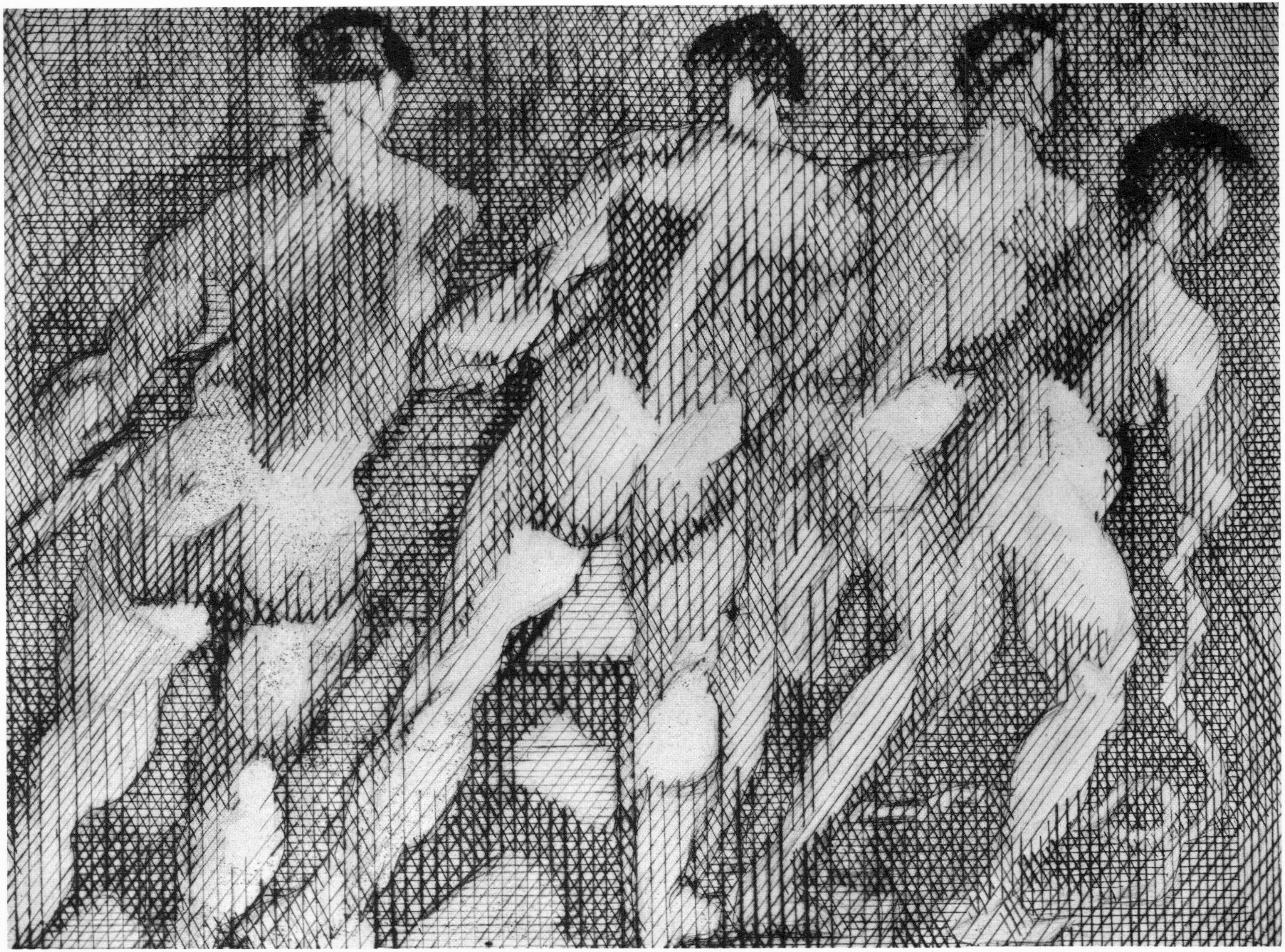

GEORGE BINET GALLERY

PAUL KLEE

Virgin in Tree

FEW MODERN ARTISTS have been the subject of so much speculation as has the provocative humorist and fantasist Paul Klee. Critics have minutely traced and analyzed his evolution from a traditionalist to one of the most personal and daring masters in modern art. His pictures have been compared to the spontaneous drawings of young children, to the fantasia of the insane, and to the naïve art of primitive peoples. There are fascinating elements from all of these in his work. But we have come to recognize Klee as an extremely sophisticated draughtsman, and a humorist who charms by the sheer ingenuity of his inventions. Perhaps the most amazing faculty of Klee is his extraordinary variety—his endless range of symbolism and imagery. Few artists rival him in sheer inventiveness, and he is a master of linear composition. Even today, sixteen years after his death, critics are divided in their evaluations of his work, but his modest and ingratiating creations still have the power to seduce the beholder whenever they are shown.

Klee was born in Switzerland in 1879, the son of musicians. After a brief inner conflict over whether he should follow his parents' musical careers, he went to Munich in 1898 to study drawing. His progression was remarkable, for in the next few years he produced a splendid series of etchings, including *Virgin in Tree,* that were inspired in part by the fantastic engravings of Blake and Fuseli. In Munich he met other painters, and with several of them formed the nucleus of the famous group "The Blue Riders," whose work jarred the staid academicians of Munich and made the word "Expressionism" known throughout the world. Shortly after the first World War, Klee joined the staff of the Bauhaus, a new technical school devoted to the study of materials and design in the arts. He taught there from 1920 to 1928, and then for three years after in the Düsseldorf Academy. He left Germany in 1933 with the advent of Hitler, and returned to Switzerland where he died seven years later in 1940.

The etching *Virgin in Tree* is one of the remarkable series he made in 1903 to 1905. Although it reflects some of the contemporary fantasists, its tight precision and contour show the Central European tradition of the late fifteenth and early sixteenth centuries. This work is not typical of Klee's more abstract style after 1918. But it does show the touch of macabre humor that characterized all his work throughout his life.

ANDRÉ DERAIN

Head of a Girl

ANY DISCUSSION OF modern French art must bring immediately to mind that most Gallic of all the "School of Paris" artists, André Derain. His work is smooth and polished with a pleasing perfection, and he has been at the very center of the ever-changing pattern of French art activity for the past forty years. He was an impressionable and eager young artist when Paris was a ferment of new explorations, discoveries and controversies. He absorbed one influence after another, adopting in turn the broad, drastically simplified style of the Fauves, abandoning it for the Primitivism inspired when Negro sculpture became a vogue, and leaving that for the geometrics of Cubism. He went from manner to manner with great ease, achieving a high standard of creativeness in each fresh field. He proved he could become part of every artistic adventure and acquit himself with distinction. Today, the many facets of styles and techniques have merged into a splendid amalgam that is distinctively Derain.

Derain was born in Chatou, France, in 1880. His father was an affluent pastry cook, and sent him to the socially acceptable schools. At sixteen he left his provincial home in the north for Paris to continue his studies in architecture. He found the course so boring that he decided to become a painter instead. He entered the atelier of Carrière at first, and then pursued his variegated career that led from Cézanne to the Fauves and Cubism. He served in the first World War, and returned to become one of the most active and respected figures in the Paris world of art.

After the war, he resumed subject painting, searching in his backgrounds of Modernism to find new starting points for his style. He went back from Cézanne to El Greco and Giotto, retaining a certain directness and an almost classical hardness and clarity. His range of subject matter was as extensive as his wide range of styles, and his works include nudes, still-lifes, portraits, landscapes and religious theme-paintings. He also made excursions into printmaking, ceramics, stage design and sculpture. In every field he is Modernism's best illustration of a rich and adaptable talent achieving perfection by study and absorption, rather than by creative invention.

His lithograph *Head of a Girl* is a charming portrait, as spontaneous and in-formal as a sketch. His knowledge of the lithographic crayon is profound—a few strokes, some textural areas filled in, and we have a perceptive and completed portrait that bears a reminder of the Oriental primitiveness that has influenced his portrait style. In spite of its apparent freedom of execution, the linear structure has a tightness and a discipline that is only apparent on analysis.

PABLO PICASSO

Le Repas Frugal

No other artist in history has been so much written about during his lifetime as Picasso. Painter, sculptor, printmaker, ceramist—all facets of his manifold activities have been discussed, dissected, eulogized and criticized during his half century of frenetic creation. Because his styles and discoveries have passed in dazzling succession, his work appears to be the creation of at least six prolific artists. Without ever repeating himself, he has returned to the same themes and styles again and again, and just as consistently, has turned to the traditional art of the past for inspiration. Almost every contemporary artist has been influenced in one way or another by the art of Picasso.

Pablo Ruiz Picasso was born on October 25, 1881, in Malaga on the Mediterranean coast of Spain. His father was an art teacher in Malaga, and when Pablo was fifteen, he removed his family to Barcelona where he became a professor in the Academy of Fine Arts. Pablo began to draw as a child, receiving instruction from his father. When he was fourteen he studied at the School of Fine Arts and later at the Royal Academy in Madrid. Within a few days of his nineteenth birthday he went to Paris, and from that time on his adopted country became his spiritual as well as his actual home.

Printmaking has always fascinated Picasso. He has worked prodigiously in all media, and has created an almost incredible number of prints in each medium. The stringent demands that printmaking makes on skill, perception and expression have been challenges that he could not resist. The techniques of each medium offer irresistible opportunities for improvisation.

Le Repas Frugal was created during his first years in Paris when frugality was an omnipresent and uncomfortable bedfellow that haunted him all the time he lived in the dilapidated tenement on Montmartre that was nicknamed "the floating laundry." He lived there among poverty-stricken artists, clerks, laundresses and actors, depending upon occasional sales to petty dealers and junkmen. The frugal repast of his two gaunt figures was a depressing reality of his own daily life.

Picasso bathed his figures in deep and half shadows that highlight protruding features and cast a dramatic aura upon the sordid scene. His technique is amazing. Tones are created by an infinite number of parallel and cross-hatched lines. The rigidity of the figures invests them with a bizarre automatism heightened by the strong deeply grooved lines that outline the figures. The stark background wall, mottled by light and shade, and the crumpled foreground tablecloth serve as a proscenium for the poignantly theatrical scene. This extraordinary print by a very young man clearly presaged the genius of the mature artist.

PABLO PICASSO

Minotauromachy

EARLY IN 1935, Picasso stopped painting, and for some twenty months thereafter his creative energies found expression in printmaking. His most remarkable composition, and probably his most important print, is the *Minotauromachy*. It is rich in a personal and involved symbolism that stems from earlier works and experiences, and any attempt to analyze its various elements would require the scope of a complete monograph.

Alfred H. Barr, Jr., in his definitive book on Picasso, describes the print as follows: "The bison-headed Minotaur advances from the right, his huge right arm stretched out toward the candle held high by a little girl who stands confronting the monster fearlessly, flowers in her other hand. Between the two staggers a horse with intestines hanging from a rent in his belly. A female matador collapses across the horse's back, her breasts bared, her espada held so that the hilt seems to touch the left hand of the Minotaur while the point lies toward the horse's head and the flower girl. At the left a bearded man in a loin cloth climbs a ladder to safety, looking over his shoulder at the monster. In a window behind and above, two girls watch two doves walk on the sill. The sea with a distant sail fills the right half of the background."

Some of the symbols of this melodramatic allegory were used in the later mural, *Guernica*. Picasso himself has not attempted to explain this monumental etching that had its genesis in associations, experiences, dreams and other inhabitants of his subconscious.

116

GEORGE WESLEY BELLOWS

Anne in a Spotted Dress

SHORTLY AFTER THE turn of the century, an era of pretty pictures and slavish imitations of popular European masters, a young artist named George Bellows, physically powerful and dynamic in personality, burst upon the art scene to become the dominant leader of the artistic revolt and the most popular artist in America. Bellows, like other artists around him, was turning to the American life surrounding him, appropriating any subject for his art so long as it was vital. Bellows became the symbol of this new declaration of independence in art. He found his material in the city streets, in the prize rings, in the art colonies and in the landscapes of the Hudson. He created art that reached right into the sensibilities of the American people. And of all his work his lithographs are the greatest expressions of his genius.

He was born in Columbus, Ohio, on August 12, 1882, descended from old American stock. He attended Ohio State University, where he alternated athletic activities with drawing illustrations and cartoons for the local papers. He arrived in New York to study art in 1904 and became the pupil of the famous teacher Robert Henri. It was a fortunate choice, for Henri became a lifelong friend and champion as well as Bellows' teacher. Success came early for Bellows. At twenty-seven he was elected to the Academy, the youngest artist at the time to receive the honor. He was financially successful from the beginning, and his work was shown and bought all over the world. His lithographs were eagerly sought after and sold for very high prices, a remarkable feat at the time, for it was a period when etching was the accepted artistic medium and lithography, through abuse, was relegated to the commercial field. Against the advice of print dealers, he was determined to bring lithography back to the esteem it once had. Together with Bolton Brown, the greatest lithographic printer of his time, Bellows not only revived lithography as a fine art, but produced an amazing total of 195 lithographs in nine years, many of them worthy to be included among the world's print masterpieces. Bellows was not yet forty-three when he died in 1925, at the very height of his creative powers.

Although he created many dramatic and suspenseful lithographs that enjoy a deserved popularity because of subject and fervor of execution, I have chosen a portrait of his daughter, *Anne in a Spotted Dress,* a favorite subject that allowed all the insight of a father's love to be revealed in a tender lyrical manner. It is a graphic endearment to his own family. All of his artistry is lavished on the halo-like hairdress that frames the small and piquant face. Silvery grays and rubbed blacks create a vital interchange of color and form. The dress is sketched lightly, the dotted pattern repeating the interplay of light and dark that is carried out in the hair and face. It is a perfectly skillful rendition in lithographic terms of an exquisite piece of portraiture. Bolton Brown executed the printing with his usual meticulous technique.

119

JOSÉ CLEMENTE OROZCO

Requiem

ONE OF THE most amazing renaissances in art history has taken place in Mexico during the past thirty years. Mexican artists discarded the academic tradition-bound influence of Spanish portraiture, still-life and landscape painting, and went back to the freshness and vigor of native Indian cultural groups. This return to original sources, plus some inspiration and enthusiasm for the modern style that spread from Paris, through Europe, and to the Americas, has resulted in a body of art that ranks with the finest in the world in freshness of vision, creative power and distinctive style. Printmaking has played a major role in this renaissance, reaching and inspiring great masses of people. Mexico's finest painters and muralists are also her most noted printmakers. The outstanding master of modern Mexican art was José Clemente Orozco. When he died in 1949, art critics of the United States called him "the El Greco of Mexico" and "one of the truly great artists of our time."

The lithograph *Requiem* is a splendid exhibition of his plastic powers and his deep roots in the emotional life of his people. It stems directly from the Jalisco region, a state from which many Mexican artists have come, and where he was born in 1883. His family moved on to Guadalajara and later to Mexico City. His parents wanted him to be an agricultural engineer, and he completed training for such a career. But in 1909 he turned to art and studied at the Academy of Fine Arts. During his student days he was active in the turbulent political life of the time and his social consciousness was reflected in his work. In 1926 he went to New York where he arranged for a show of drawings. A tour of Europe followed where he absorbed the influences of Byzantine frescoes at Rome and Ravenna. When he returned he received mural commissions from Dartmouth College, Pomona College and the New School in New York. Official honors from his own country came later than recognition of his talents in the United States. He was finally awarded Mexico's highest honor, the prize given to the nation's outstanding cultural exponent.

Requiem was made in 1928, and is a departure from the usual violence that filled his art. It is a tender and compassionate study of five praying women mourning before an altar for their men slain in some battle of Mexico's devastating civil wars. The bowed backs are eloquent in their projection of grief. The darkness of the altar, relieved only by two slim white candles, is an effective background for the foreground figures. Gray, white and black areas filter through the scene as rhythmically as musical counterpoint. The intense emotionalism and masterful execution make this work one of the most poignant expressions of anguish in the history of the print.

KARL SCHMIDT-ROTTLUFF

The Three Kings

In 1905, the year in which the Fauves rose to prominence in Paris, three young disciples of Edvard Munch founded a group called "Die Brucke" (The Bridge). The artists—Kirchner, Heckel and Schmidt-Rottluff—were fascinated by primitive painting and sculpture, particularly the creations of the native artists of Africa and Oceania. The artists of this new group called all the refined and complicated aspects of the world about them superficial and unimportant. Their main interest was in the bases of human character and conduct, and these they conceived as violent and unpleasant. They tried to portray these passions and emotions in as outspoken a manner as possible.

Karl Schmidt-Rottluff was one of the most militant in the group. He was born in Saxony in 1884 and went to Dresden to study architecture. He found that he preferred painting, and was on his way to becoming an Impressionist when he met Kirchner and Heckel. With them he frequented the cabarets and music halls and depicted this milieu at a level of intensity which is rarely reached in the ordinary routine of daily events. The exoticism of Gauguin, with his romantic-symbolic attitude toward nature, also attracted them, and they unsuccessfully tried to bring to their northern home the blazing warmth of Gauguin's equatorially conceived landscapes.

Schmidt-Rottluff's personal style was founded first on Hodler, Munch and Van Gogh, but was later modified by elements from stained-glass windows of medieval German cathedrals and the primitive German woodcuts of the fifteenth and sixteenth centuries. He eagerly embraced the technique of the woodcut because it afforded bold and uncomplicated effects, completely appropriate for his intense religious subjects and his analytical delvings into the subconscious, newly discovered by Freud.

In the powerful woodcut *The Three Kings,* made in 1917, there is a deliberate coarsening of his deeply cut lines, a simplification of form, and dramatic contrast between black and white. The faces are extremely stylized, a characteristic that appears in African and Oceanic sculpture and ritual masks. Although Schmidt-Rottluff was an accomplished artist, it is interesting to note that the lack of refinement of technique he has used corresponds to an early stage in the development of the woodcut, and he chose even to reduce the possibilities of so limited a style. It is a splendid example of the work that later led to Expressionism and its desire to penetrate to the essence of things.

ANDRÉ DUNOYER DE SEGONZAC

Versailles, la Menagerie

FROM THE VERY first time Segonzac worked on a copper plate, after just a single lesson from the engraver Laboureur, he instinctively seemed to possess all of the secrets of the etcher's craft. The etching needle seemed to be a natural continuation of his nervous system, communicating every thought and image to the copper that his eye delineated and his brain defined. In the long years devoted to the etcher's art, Segonzac has created at least a thousand plates, many of them powerful nudes and fine sport subjects, but his chief love and his finest achievement is the landscape. These he models with the calm precision and the patient discipline of his master, Cézanne.

Segonzac was born in Boussy-Saint-Antoine, France, in 1884, of a very old and distinguished family. In school he specialized in Oriental languages, and after graduation he went to the North African desert to study the dialects of Sudanese tribes. But the visual rather than the auricular won out, and he left for Paris in 1902 to study art. He worked at the studios of Merson, Laurens and Blanche. He took little part in the ferment of the Left Bank where the Fauves and later the Cubists were erupting. His enthusiasms centered on Douanier Rousseau, Cézanne and the earlier masters. He fought and was decorated in the first World War, and then left Paris for the country of his father's ancestors, the landscapes of Gascony, where his love for nature found expression in his paintings and etchings.

Segonzac works on the copper direct from nature. His etching needle immediately captures the scene visualized, and that practice invests all his prints with a marvelous sense of spontaneity, a wonderful feeling for light, and his varied and exciting line. No other artist has ever translated the atmosphere of the south of France with such vividness and economy of means. Examine the etching *Versailles, la Menagerie* for its exquisite sense of serenity, and Segonzac's ability to convey the volume and weight of figures with just a few lines. It is a splendid affirmation of perfect communion between man and nature.

124

DIEGO RIVERA

Sleep

JEAN CHARLOT ONCE wrote: "If I had to choose, out of the whole panorama of the Mexican graphic arts, a single print, I would not choose either the biggest print or the loudest, impressive as is the Mexican version of both." Diego Rivera, stormy petrel of Mexican art, has contributed his share of loud and impressive prints, many of which rank with the finest graphic art in the world. He is the gadfly of Mexican art and life, constantly involved in national controversies, and serving as a stimulus to the intellectual activity of his country. His genius, enthusiasm, ideas and ideals have helped fashion a truly indigenous art of contemporary Mexico. The lithograph chosen to represent his work, *Sleep,* is neither loud nor large. It is a tender, lyrical study that has no great profoundity of statement and conception, but it is a part of life that has touched the artist deeply and with compassion. It is a life ideal, an image of beauty drawn from his native roots.

Few people realize that Rivera has been a prolific creator of art for fifty-five years. He was born in Guanajuato in 1886, and as a boy he studied in the San Carlos Academy. In 1907 he went to Spain and studied under Eduardo Chicharro, then Director of the Spanish Academy of Painting. Later he traveled through Europe, absorbing the influences of Cézanne, Picasso, Derain, Braque and Klee. He allied himself closely with the French School during the eighteen years he spent in Europe. When he returned to Mexico he joined other artists in forming the Painters Syndicate, and soon became the leader in mural painting. He worked on many of the public buildings of Mexico and also executed murals in San Francisco, Detroit and New York. In 1931 the Museum of Modern Art of New York presented an exhibition of his work, and in 1949 the National Institute of Fine Arts in Mexico honored him with a retrospective "fifty years" exhibition. His reputation as one of the outstanding artists of this century is secure.

Rivera has assimilated a wealth of pictorial experience and emerged with a distinctive style that is personal and strong. *Sleep* is typical of the realist approach that has been criticized by some Modernists. But a dissection of the figures and textures of this print will show that its composition had its genesis in the theories of analytical Cubism. Its interpenetrating planes and the juxtaposition of textures and forms stem directly from the Cubism of his early Paris years. The Modernist influence has deep roots in his expression, but to that he has added the ancient wisdom of his own forbears and has emerged with a truly American style.

127

JOHN TAYLOR ARMS

Sunshine on Stone

IN EARLY TWENTIETH-CENTURY America, worship and emulation of the Gothic was the order of the day. Architects were in the midst of a fervent Gothic revival and Gothic spires were rising on the campuses of colleges all over the country. John Taylor Arms studied and matured during this revival, and became its greatest graphic interpreter and the acknowledged master of the architectural print.

Born in the District of Columbia in 1887, Arms studied architecture at Princeton and later at the Massachusetts Institute of Technology. He graduated in 1911 and practiced for five years. The first World War intervened and he served a term in the Navy. After his discharge he decided to forsake architecture and give his entire attention to graphic art. Instead of creating the buildings of the present, he would devote himself to interpreting the classics of architecture of the past. For him, as for others of his generation, the greatest achievements of architecture of the past were the soaring spires, the flying buttresses, the magnificent "sermons in stone" which were the buildings of the Gothic era.

Until his death in 1953, Arms dedicated his prodigious talents to recording the glories of the Gothic in hundreds of etchings and engravings. He reveled in the varied richness of Gothic façades which he delineated with a technical perfection polished almost to the point of virtuosity. He was particularly attracted to the tonal variations inherent in old stone, and he made the most of every nuance of light and dark reflected from its variegated surfaces. His work became a careful, minute and amazingly accurate rendering of every detail of the Gothic masterpieces he engraved.

The etching *Sunshine on Stone* epitomizes the whole of Arms' graphic creations. In subject, in technique and in conception, it is the summation of Arms' esthetic. In this print his emphasis is on the tonal values of the scene in which luminous sunlight pours down on the irregular lines of the sidewalk and creates a chiaroscuric interplay between the dark masses on the side buildings and the shafts of light on the slender spires of the cathedral. Every minute variation of light and shade and each decorative detail of the building is rendered with exquisite craftsmanship.

In his published *Credo,* Arms wrote: "To define my concept of a work of art, I believe it to be an emotion profoundly and poignantly sensed, expressed with nobility and humility and in terms of knowledge and skill, and contributing in some degree to the sum total of human enjoyment, inspiration and understanding." His art and his activities in support of that art bear impressive testament to the fulfillment of his *Credo.*

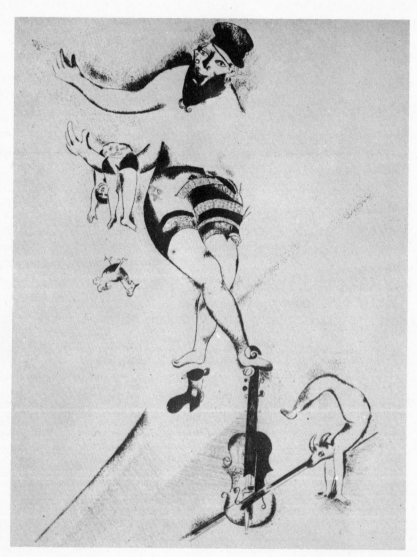

BUCHHOLZ GALLERY

MARC CHAGALL

Acrobat with Violin

AN EXTRAORDINARY ROMANTICIST, Marc Chagall has for many years held art lovers spellbound by the charm of his uniquely personal poetic imagery expressed in the conventions of true folk art. He has created a fantastic world, a fairy-tale universe, viewing his dream creatures with a child's innocence of eye, but creating them with a sustained skill and Oriental sumptuousness that is unique in contemporary art. Chagall's strange world of freely floating figures, wondrous birds and beasts and sensual symbolism is a prefiguration of the dreamscapes of the Surrealists. In all his work the fervent ecstasy of the Chassidic Jew—his religious inheritance—is strongly apparent. Although his art is not generally emulated, his influence on modern art is marked and profound.

Chagall was born in Vitebsk, Russia, in 1889, one of ten children. In his art he has returned to the locale of his childhood again and again. At the age of seventeen he went to St. Petersburg where he studied at the newly organized school of Leon Bakst. It was the only art school in Russia where currents of West European art were allowed to circulate. At twenty he left Bakst to go to Paris where he entered into the hectic activity of the art capital. His paintings of the Russian ghetto and portraits of aristocratic Jewish types caused excitement at the Independent shows and established his reputation in Europe. He returned to Vitebsk on the eve of the first World War and was forced to remain in Russia for the next eight years by closed borders. He started an art school in Vitebsk, exhibited at the Moscow Art Salon, and was, for a brief period, Minister of Arts during the Russian Revolution. He also became stage designer for the State Jewish Theater. He left Russia in 1922 for Berlin, where he helped form the Expressionist movement, and then went on to Paris where he continued to work and exhibit with the great French moderns. In 1941 Chagall came to New York where he was active in printmaking and stage designing for the ballet. At the end of the war he returned to France where he now lives and works.

Chagall has executed close to five hundred subjects in graphic media. His career as a printmaker is closely linked to the publisher Vollard who commissioned many prints as book illustrations. His early prints were woodcuts and lithographs, but he later found that etching and drypoint were his true media. He has also created unique combinations of media in a single print. Perhaps his greatest work was done as illustrations for the Bible. The etching *Acrobat with Violin* is a true reflection of his gift for fantasy. The bizarre juxtaposition of figures and his complete disregard for formal composition is dramatically illustrated in this plate. It is a combination of etching and drypoint done with a sensitive eye for the rhythmic effects of black and white.

JEAN CHARLOT

First Steps

CHARLOT IS ONE of the most active missionaries of the art of printmaking today. His own splendid lithographs, lectures, teachings and writings have opened up new vistas of understanding and appreciation for the print both in the United States and Mexico. This French-born Mexican arrived in Mexico at a time when prints were beneath the concern of native artists. His manifold activities gave impetus to a revival of printmaking which became Mexico's liveliest art form.

A Charlot print is distinctive and immediately recognizable. His squarish sculptural figures are a delightful blending of Mayan art and contemporary sophistication. They are, as he puts it, "a re-creation in terms of living Mayas." Albert Reese, in his book *American Prize Prints of the Twentieth Cenutry,* writes that the artist has "an extraordinary grasp of sculptural form and the sense of design which fuses all elements, human and inanimate, into a powerful dynamic entity." His prints are truly graphic ambassadors interpreting Mexicans to the Americans.

Charlot was born in Paris in 1898, of a family which included French, Russian and Aztec ancestors. In 1921 he came to Mexico and quickly became a participant in the art renaissance by creating both mural paintings and prints. Since 1929 he has been practically a commuter between the United States and Mexico. He has worked in many American cities and taught in at least a dozen American schools. He has been active in artists' organizations in both countries, and has written several volumes of art criticism. For the past few years he has been teaching and working in Hawaii, absorbing the old art and customs of that civilization. It should be interesting to see the transmutation of ethnic group characteristics into one. But, as he says, both are similar in many ways, "except that the Hawaiians are a happy people and the Mexican Indians are sad."

The lithograph *First Steps* is a typical and charming print. It is one of Charlot's familiar subjects—the kitchen, the mother, the child, the Sunday dress, and this, a child's first steps. It is a plastic conception, modeled three-dimensionally in the round, and his forms are squarish, firm and strong. The child's face is stylized, as are most of his faces, and conveys the essence of all children's faces. The design is simple, as befits the subject, and on the whole it is a decorative and ingratiating print that wins instant response and favor on sight.

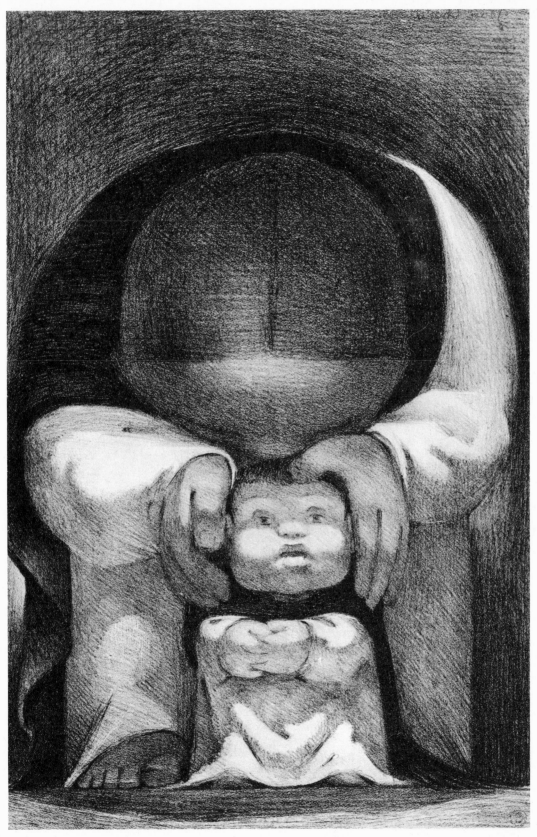

ARMIN LANDECK

Roof Tops, 14th Street

MANY ARTISTS HAVE been bewitched by the color and personality of a city. The brittle beauty of Paris haunted Meryon and Utrillo after him. Piranesi was obsessed by the ruins of Rome and devoted his life to engraving them. Armin Landeck has a wise and understanding love for the streets of New York—her alleyways, roofs and houses, the soot-encrusted beauty of old brownstones, and sidewalks lit by streetlights. These are the motifs that he returns to again and again. Mark Van Doren described Landeck's themes: "The New York that shows itself in them . . . has the air of never having expected to be seen by any man as Armin Landeck sees it. It is seen in that aspect of eternity which conceals neither the triumphs nor the ravages of change. . . ." It is that part of New York that is never apparent to the casual beholder but remains a challenge to the perceptive eye. Many of his finest prints are studies of his immediate neighborhood, thus proving the truth of Renoir's retort when he was told that Gauguin had gone to Tahiti. "One can paint as well in the Batignolles," Renoir said.

Armin Landeck was born in Crandon, Wisconsin, in 1905. He studied at Columbia University and started printmaking in 1928. He is one of the few printmakers ever admitted to membership in The National Institute of Arts and Letters. His early architectural training is apparent in the distinctive style he created. He uses strong rigid vertical and horizontal lines to delineate both form and tone, and weaves them into an intricate linear network that is technically brilliant. This dynamic linear approach is eminently suitable for his atmospheric scenes of streets and buildings bathed by streetlight and moonlight. The source of illumination filters through his open-lined forms, investing them with an eerie chiaroscuro that reminds one of Piranesi.

In the etching *Roof Tops, 14th Street,* Landeck has used his favorite locale, downtown New York, and his favorite motifs, roofs, walls, windows and moonlight. His calligraphy is severe in its conception of diagonals, verticals and horizontals, but there is no feeling of stiffness, no unpleasant rigidity. His skillful interplay of strong shadows and moonlight create a plasticity that gives his scene pictorial interest and saves it from the monotony of pure abstract design. Landeck's imagination has endowed his inanimate subject with dignity and character and given it a vitality that is the very essence of art. The beholder becomes a participant in Landeck's reaction to his small, but so well understood, universe, and, in doing so, shares the miracle that the artist has conceived. It is this sense of identification which Landeck can inspire that assures him of an important place in the graphic arts of our time.

135

INDEX OF ARTISTS